THE BRIDGES OF CREEMORE MILLS
1832-1871

by

Helen Emmett Blackburn

Two Old Chinese Proverbs

*To forget one's ancestors is to be like a brook without a source,
a tree without a root.*

Even the palest ink is more reliable than the most retentive memory.

From Families Vol. 38, no. 2, May, 1999

Blackberry Press
c/o Helen Blackburn
R.R. #1
Nottawa, ON
L0M 1P0

Canadian Cataloguing in Publication Data

Blackburn, Helen Emmett, 1936-
    The Bridges of Creemore Mills 1832-1871

Includes bibliographical references and index.
ISBN 0-9685337-0-1

1. Creemore (Ont.) - History. I. Title.

FC3099.C733B52 1999 971.3'17   C99-931696-6
F1059.5.C733B52 1999

Cover Photo
This photograph was taken circa 1900 but gives a glimpse of earlier
times. The mill was built many years previously and the two wooden
bridges show the style of the 1800s. The one on the left crossed the Mad
River and the smaller one on the right was over the mill race that flowed
to the mill and powered it.

Produced by Creemore Echo Productions, Creemore, Ontario

THE BRIDGES OF CREEMORE MILLS
1832-1871

TABLE OF CONTENTS

THE SURVEY OF NOTTAWASAGA

It is hard to imagine our local landscape in the grip of the primeval forest, with tree trunks as wide as the span of our arms, fallen, moss-covered logs, and free roaming wildlife. In our ancestors' quest to take over this treasure it was necessary to divide it up in an orderly fashion. For this reason surveyors were the first to organize the space and to map it.

The forests of today in Southern Ontario are much different than those of the early 1800s. Most of the huge trees and forest areas were cut down by 1900, so, at most, our woods and swamps have been developing for a century or less. It is true, there were spots where the Petun Indian clearings of the early 1600s meant trees were only 175 or 200 years old but, on the whole, the trees had been growing and dying undisturbed since the last ice age.

There are a few descriptions of treks through the Nottawasaga area before settlement encroached. Samuel Thompson wrote <u>Reminiscences of a Canadian Pioneer</u> to tell about his experiences in what is now Ontario in the 1830s. Somewhere west of the Nottawasaga River in 1833 we come upon Thompson walking from Barrie to Sunnidale. This is how he describes what he saw. "For some miles further, the forest consisted of Norway and white pine, almost unmixed with any other timber. There is something majestic in these vast and thickly-set labyrinths of brown columnar stems averaging a hundred and fifty feet in height, perhaps, and from one to five feet in thickness making a traveller feel somewhat like a Lilliputian Gulliver in a field of Brobdignagian wheat. It is singular to observe the effect of an occasional gust of wind in such situations. It might not even fan your cheek; but you feel a low surging sound, like the moaning of breakers in a calm sea, which gradually increases to a loud boisterous roar, still seemingly at a great distance; the branches remain in perfect repose, you can find no evidence of a stirring breeze, till looking perpendicularly upwards, you are astonished to see some patriarchal giant close at hand six yards round and sixty high which alone has caught the breeze, waving its huge fantastic arms wildly at a dizzy height above your head." [1]

A little later he describes the trees in Grey County. "Oak, elm, beech, butternut, ash and maple seem to vie with each other in the size of their stems and the spread of their branches. In our own clearing in St. Vincent the axe men considered that five of these great forest kings would occupy an acre of ground, leaving little space for younger trees or underbrush.

"I once saw a white or waincot oak that measured fully twelve feet in circumference at the butt, and eighty feet clear of branches."[2]

Tales of bears and wolves abound. In most cases these are true stories, but it is wise to consider that these types of tales often grow with each telling. In The Pioneers of Old Ontario the author tells us, "In the summer of 'thirty-seven, bears were almost as thick as blackberries, and the tracks left by wolves were as common as sheep tracks now." [3]

In Nottawasaga: The Outburst of the Iroquois is a tale of wolves. "When the Northern railway was being built from Toronto to Collingwood...a young lad was working on the construction with his yoke of oxen, just two miles north of what is now Stayner. About twelve o'clock at night, watchmen awoke him and told him that his oxen had broken out of the inclosure. He hurriedly dressed, lit his lantern, and started on the homeward trail. When in the middle of that dense woods, to his horror, he heard the howling pack of wolves evidently on the trail to the Georgian bay. The deer in autumn usually went down from Osprey Township and Collingwood mountain to the more sheltered woods along the Georgian bay, the Nottawasaga River, Sunnidale and Flos, and thither the wolves followed them. The boy climbed a small tree and sat among the branches where he remained until morning. Several of the wolves turned aside from the trail, sniffed around the tree, then in unison gave a blood curdling howl like a legion of fiends from the inferno, and followed the pack. The oxen went home another path and thus cheated the hungry wolves out of a fine feast of beef-steak and tenderloin." [4]

The demand for more land and the desire of the government for revenue from Clergy Reserves and Crown lands necessitated that more areas be surveyed. Into the forest of kings and giants and bears and wolves came Thomas Kelly and his troupe of ten surveyors. Kelly had passed muster with the government authorities and was assigned the job of surveying much of Sunnidale and Nottawasaga.

Before moving along with the marking of roads and lots it is necessary to retreat a few years. On October 17, 1818, five principal men of the Ojibway nation signed a treaty to relinquish the land they held between

Lake Ontario and Georgian Bay. This tract contained 1,592,000 acres and for that the chiefs received 1,200 Pounds annually. It is not stated how long this amount was presented.[5] The government then lost no time in mapping out townships for settlement.[6] While information is available on how a township was surveyed, Nottawasaga, for example, it is not clear how the boundaries for each township were decided.

Kelly obviously knew, for in the fall of 1832 he conducted a survey of a section of Sunnidale Township and was able to define the boundaries before moving on to Nottawasaga. Nottawasaga was not Nottawasaga then, but Merlin in the south and Java in the north. The word, Nottawasaga, comes from the Ojibway words, Nottoway Sague, which they named the southern part of Georgian Bay.[7] Merlin took in the southern 32 lots and Java the rest, an area too small to make a viable township. In 1833 the Surveyor-General decided that the two smaller townships should become one and the names changed.[8]

What were Kelly's instructions on the survey? He followed the rules laid down in an 1829 Order-in-Council sponsored by the Acting Surveyor-General, William Chewett. This provided for a 2400 Acres Township. This meant that there would be rectangles within the township, approximately 2 1/2 miles by 1 3/4 miles subdivided into 12 lots of 200 acres. An unsurveyed line was left between alternate concessions.[9]

But, now, let's go back to Kelly. The information about his survey comes directly from his journal which is in the Archives of Ontario.[10] It is a small notebook, probably of a size that would fit into a pocket. It begins, "Diery [sic] for the Township of Merlin." Someone later crossed out"Merlin" and wrote in "Nottawasaga." On Tuesday, October 16th, 1832, he wrote, "The following men who had been with me on the survey of part of the Township of Sunnidale continued also in this Township. 1. James McKowan, chain bearer, 2. Rodrick McDermot, chain bearer, 3. Pat Bunan, 4. Timothy O'Connor, 5. John O'Neill, 6. Peter Fingtiton, 7. William Hartry, 8. Pat Howard, 9. John McDonnell, 10, James Heemy. Surveyed the eastern Line of Merlin from the middle of the 14th lot to the end of the 18th Lot. The day fine."

Day by day he made his way, marking out the rectangles of 2400 acres prescribed by the Acting Surveyor-General. On Wednesday, October 24th they surveyed "from near the end of the 5th lot to the beginning of the 1st lot between 2nd and 3rd con. The day fine." This is how the work would go: the ax men would go ahead cutting down trees and saplings to clear a line-of-sight. A compass was used to keep the lines going in the right direction. The chain men would then measure off the front of the property lots using a surveyor's chain. This chain was in rods, a chain measuring four rods.[11] Corner posts, cut from small trees, were driven into the soil and the appropriate lot numbers marked on both sides.

Kelly made no comments about the lots that now comprise Creemore. He might have remarked that it was stony or that the river was hard to cross but no such remarks exist. Friday, October 26th, they "[s]urveyed from the beginning of the first Lot between the 4th and 5th con. [T]o the end of the 8th Lot. On this day four of my party go out to Kempenfelt Bay for provisions." The end of the 8th Lot would bring them somewhere near the present day area of Collingwood and Elizabeth or Caroline Streets in Creemore. The next day they continued to the end of the 12th Lot.

The surveying went well, blessed as they were with fine weather. They worked six days and rested on Sunday. Suddenly, in November everything went wrong. On Tuesday, November 6th Kelly wrote, "About one o'clock on this morning Rodrick McDermot a native of the County of Sligo in Ireland and nephew to Mr John McDermot of York died. He complained of illness for about ten days. It was about the 30th Oct'r that one of the men made me acquainted with his sickness which was occasioned by a kind of Dysentery. I noticed him to have reduced much in his strength. I ordered that he should stay in our kind of tent, in as much as the circumstances of our business would admit until he would be fully recovered. [I]t was about 8 o'clock on the evening previous to his death before we got back from Surveying. He said he felt unpleasant at being alone and thought he might be able to go out on the ensuing morning and requested some Fryed Mate [fried meat] might be prepared for Supper as it was customary for us to Boil our Pork on almost all occasions. He ate his supper considerably better than he usually [did] (as for some time I noticed him to be delicate in his appetite) and we went to Bed. [H]e was heard at about 12 o'clock to speak to Pat Howard, who, being tired after the day, made no reply. I awoke in about an hour after and heard him give two or three heavy sighs. I called him by his name but got no answer. I called still louder and got none. I then awoke James McKowan who lay near and turning him on his Back found him in the very act of expiring. He was well conducted and modest in every respect that I could know, an excellent character. We had a heavy fall of snow from the Hour

INTRODUCTION

Me? Read detective novels? Never. It is more fun to be the detective. Instead of hiding behind hedges or furtively listening to conversations on public pay phones, I openly ask people questions, search through ancient books and papers in libraries and archives and tread down paths long forgotten.

The main reason for producing this book is to share my enthusiasm for local history and as a motive on a higher plane, to remind us that our forebears struggled to survive and our good fortune has its roots in those difficulties that were overcome. Perhaps we quickly think of physical problems: marauding wild animals, cold drafty houses and hard labour. There were also legal and financial worries such as whether there would be money to pay the mortgage in a cashless society, or whether, indeed, the land the settlers were on was legally theirs. Rules for ownership through settlement duties were constantly shifting. So let us appreciate what they gave us.

We are blessed with numerous accounts of our past in local histories and newspapers going back at least one hundred years. These tales, carefully saved, are the starting points for research in this day and age. Every time the story was told many facts were embroidered and changed. We are very fortunate to have many primary sources available now, especially on microfilm, that can correct some strange ideas that have proliferated. I know that I have been one of the proliferators and I apologize for misinforming you at times. I have tried very hard to check my sources, sometimes several times and from several places. No doubt I'm still making errors but I promise to correct them in the future.

Many people today are interested in their family history and so I am including a detailed index to help those of you who are involved in this fascinating hobby. As well, my sources are noted so you can continue your searches more readily.

So, go forth, dear readers, and make your way down the path through the primeval forest to Creemore where bridges crossed the Mad River and made the village the hub of the local area, tying us together in a well-knit community.

THANK YOU!

This is going to sound like Oscar Night on TV. No, no, I don't mean I hope I win a prize. It's the "Thank you's" that will be the same as on that popular night. Truly, no man (or woman) is an island and it would be impossible for me to research local history without so many kind and obliging friends. Some people have just answered a question or two, others have helped a whole lot, and many have given encouragement and have shown interest. Here's the big list and I hope I haven't missed anyone.

The staff at the Ontario Archives, particularly Serge Paquet; the staff at the Simcoe County Archives; the people I talked to by phone at the Anglican, Baptist and Presbyterian Archives; the staff at the Dufferin County Archives; the librarians at Creemore and Collingwood Public Libraries; the staff at the Clearview Municipal Office; the staff at Collingwood Museum; Byron Wesson, Nottawasaga Valley Conservation Authority; Allan Day, Ministry of Natural Resources; John Brillinger; Ed and Joan Maynard; Gary French; Rev. Bullock; Agnes Douglas; Eileen Giffen; Marie Talbot; Carman Gowan; Ross Fraser; Doreen McDermid; Jim Steed; Eleanor Wines; Bob Stephenson; Melissa Campbell; Donna Lowe; Joan Wilson; Elsie Agar; Bill Timmons; Winton Schneider; John Smart; Don Carmichael; Michelle Matthews; Georgi Denison, Julie Fletcher; Della Whitlam; Rev. Whitlam; Lawrence Montgomery; Chris and Pat Raible; Jack Heslip; Barry Gough; Gertie Gowan; Colleen Stamp; Eileen Crysler; members of the Creemore Writers' Group; Donald and Carolyn Webster; Mary West (researcher in California), and the person I spoke to at the Orange Lodge Headquarters, Toronto.

I can't forget my mother, Alice Emmett, and my grandmother, Alice Webster, who recorded so much local history and were the kind of people who never threw anything out. My father, Bill Emmett, and grandfather, Frank Webster, loved a good story, both to tell and to listen to. I grew up nourished by all those interesting stories of the past. My husband, Gordon Blackburn, my sons, Frank and Alex Hargrave, and my sister, Ruth Hughes, have all been kind enough to listen to my enthusiastic ramblings about my latest discovery. A big thank you to them and to everyone!

he died until near night. We had much difficulty in making Boards and digging his Grave. We buried him on the 19th Lot in the 4th con of Appointed Pat Bunan chain man."

There was snow and sleet all the next day but on Thursday they went on surveying. The survey complete, Kelly and his men returned to York County.

A further comment, not particularly complimentary, may be found in Hunter's History of Simcoe County.[12] "Thomas Kelly made a survey of the Township of Nottawasaga in 1832, and completed a map of it, Feb. 27th, 1833, as far north as lot 32 (inclusive) in the first eleven concessions, the last, or twelfth, being omitted. There has been a tradition among the older settlers of the township itself, how that a whiskey bottle bore a conspicuous part in the survey on this occasion, so that, if not the surveyor himself, at least some of his axe men or helpers were too much addicted to the flowing bowl to make a good job of staking out the lots. The map he left for posterity to ponder looks all right, yet we are reminded to be cautious about what we see on paper. Be the circumstances what they may, Charles Rankin, under instructions from the Surveyor-General, dated March 23rd, 1833, re-surveyed parts and completed the survey of, it more especially the northern end and western parts, in the ensuing summer."

Rankin's diary is available for study and it reveals no indication of poor surveying on Kelly's part. He surveyed the northern part of the township and the incompleted western concessions. His diary includes much more commentary on the trees, the streams and the land formations.[13]

NOTES
   1. Reminiscences of a Canadian Pioneer. p. 48.
   2. See above, pp. 98-99.
   3. The Pioneers of Old Ontario, p. 54.
   4. Nottawasaga: The Outburst of the Iroquois. pp. 80-81.
   5. A History of Simcoe County, pp. 14-15.
   6. See above, p. 35.
   7. See above, p. 13.
   8. See above, p. 47.
   9. "The Land Surveys of Ontario 1750-1980," Cartographica.
   10. Thomas Kelly's Diary. Microfilm number MS 924, Reel 18. Archives of Ontario.

11. For those who have not had to do elementary school math problems using rods, it is 161/2 feet.

12. <u>A History of Simcoe County,</u> page 47.

13. Rankin, "Field Notes, Notes, Nottawasaga," Office of the Surveyor General, Peterborough, ON.

THE EARLY LAND GRANTS

In the rush of day-to-day living we like to think that life was simpler "way back then," that people went to bed weary but content. To be sure, they had to cut down monster trees, build their own homes and produce their own food. On the other hand, they had security, no taxes to speak of, and a peaceful world to live in. That is what we like to think, but on investigation we find it isn't so.

To begin with, most of the first settlers were refugees from the American Revolution with their own memories of atrocities. Britain, ruling our part of North America, welcomed them as loyal citizens. They would bring development and prosperity and in case of invasion from the United States, fight to remain British. These people were to receive free land grants and other assistance.

From the beginning there was no end of trouble with land policy. The settlers never knew whether they had rights to their grants or just what they were supposed to do to obtain the land. The governments kept changing its minds and with the poor communication of the pioneer days, confusion reigned.

A summary here might help you to understand what people went through in their desire to have a piece of property of their own. Although Nottawasaga was surveyed in 1832, there were very few people moving in for ten years or so. The information comes from a book called The Land Policies of Upper Canada. [1]

The heads of families fleeing the American Revolution and its aftermath were to receive land grants. The understanding of these Loyalists, however, was that each of their children were also entitled to free land. The government decided that would be a good policy and then later changed its mind and rescinded the order. At different times fees were to be paid to receive clear title, at other times there were no fees, and then sometimes only for a select group.

In addition to the obligation of a fee levied from time to time, there was also confusion over settlement duties. These might include clearing and fencing five acres out of each hundred, and building a habitable dwelling. The regulations were often changed and sometimes meant only clearing half the road allowance and a strip along the front of the property. Another problem with settlement duties was enforcing them. An inspector had to be found to travel into the hinter land to check the properties and be paid for his efforts.

The centre for land administration was York, now Toronto, and for a while, those seeking title to property were obliged to travel there. As you can imagine this was no easy task as the settler had to walk most of the way. District Land Boards were set up in various centres, but later abolished when other plans were formulated to improve the system.

Following fast on the heels of the Loyalists were more people, both from the United States and Britain. The question of how to treat them brought more controversy. There was a fear that the Americans were importing ideas of democracy and the Colonial Government favoured a rich, landed upper class to provide examples of the correct values to the lower class. The problem was that the British immigrants were often poverty stricken with no means of buying land, but the Americans came with the cash and the necessary survival skills for life in the bush. As a result this new group was treated the same as the Loyalists although sometimes they weren't.

Into all this confusion, as usual, came speculators. How to stop their tying up tracts of land was another problem and it seemed that no matter what was done, the plans were sabotaged. Also immobilizing a large acreage were the Crown Lands and the Clergy Reserves, a full two sevenths of the total. They could be purchased but the regulations were constantly changing. It was little wonder that squatters set themselves up wherever they were able.

As you can imagine, there was much dissatisfaction and grumbling among the people. The 1837 Rebellion in Upper Canada was partially an outburst of their concern. It surely was a worry to wonder whether several years of clearing land would all be in vain.

Land in the Creemore-to-be area was granted after 1832, but there was little action there for over ten years. The survey of Nottawasaga meant there were more lots to fulfill the promise of land grants to Loyalists and veterans of the war of 1812-14.

As you will see, lots in the Creemore area were assigned, but not taken up. This information comes from a microfilm in the Archives of Ontario.[2] Perhaps the old soldiers were already established elsewhere as twenty years had passed since the war. Possibly the Loyalists were in the same situation. However, surprisingly, there was a lone settler, and maybe his brother, sitting on Creemore land before the influx in the 1840s. Previous histories of the area have given no indication of any settlers before the forties.

In the Nottawasaga Land Records there is a certificate which reads, "To all to whom these presents may come: This may certify, that I Nicholas Lake being returned by Mr. Wellesley Richey, to the Government, as an actual settler on Lot No. 9 in the fourth Concession of the Township of Nottawasaga, under Israel Bowerman and Archelaus Tupper, do hereby agree that John McDonald Esq. may be allowed to Locate such claim for Land on the said Lot, as he may be entitled to Locate..." The rest is legal wording. It is signed by William Lake, Nicholas Lake, Israel Bowerman, Archaelaus Tupper, and Samuel (last name indistinct) and dated Jan. 28th, 1837.[3]

The Lakes are also noted on a wonderful hand-drawn map found in Simcoe County Archives. It was drawn by Archelaus Tupper and dated May 5th, 1837. The lots have the settlers' names on them and Nicholas Lake is clearly shown as having the north-west corner of lot 9, concession 4. This would probably be the land bounded by Collingwood, Wellington, and Mary Streets and County Road 9 in today's Creemore. Across the corner the land is noted as being owned by William Lake.[4] You may notice that the date of the map is later than the agreement to give up his land by Nicholas Lake. The map probably shows the area as it was explored by Tupper the previous year or two.

As mentioned above, the lots in the Creemore area were granted to Militia men from the War of 1812-14 and to Loyalists from the United States. John McDonald (more about him later) obtained the land by assignment. This meant that his name was not the original one on the land records but an agreement was made that he could have the lots. It is not clear whether he paid for them or not, as the regulations changed so often. He may have obtained them for nothing and accepted the responsibility and expense of bringing in settlers. The information about the change in ownership follows.

South half of lot 7 in the 4th concession: grant to John McDonald, assignee of Clarissa Marsh, the assignee of Bernard Smith, a discharged soldier from the 104th regiment, 10 Jan. 18?3.[5]

North half of Lot 7 in the 4th concession: grant to John McDonald, assignee of David Haslett, a discharged soldier from the 27th Regiment of (name indistinct). 26th November, 1840.[6]

Lot 9, Concession 4: Israel Tripp of the Township of Sophiaburg, received a militia grant in the Township of Brock which was changed to Nottawasaga in November , 1837, and then to McDonald in 1843.[7]

South half of lot 9 in the 4th concession: grant to John McDonald, assignee of Jonathan Wilde, the assignee of Artemas W. Cushman, a private in the Light Dragoons of the 1st Rgt. Of Addington Militia during the late war. 30th August, 1842.[8]

North half of lot 9 in the 4th concession: grant to John McDonald, the assignee of William Rorke, the assignee of Israel Tripp, a private in a troup of Dragoons of the 1st Rgt. Of Prince Edward Militia during the late war. 27th September, 1842.[9]

Lot 7 in the 5th concession: grant to John McDonald, the assignee of Clarissa Marsh, the assignee of William Lindsay, son of James Lindsay, an U.E Loyalist. 10th October, 1842.[10]

Lot 10 in the 5th concession: grant to John McDonald, assignee of Randy Munro, the son of Daniel Munro of the Township of Yonge, an U.E. Loyalist 5th May, 1842.[11]

There are no records in this microfilm for the south half of lot 10 in the 4th concession or for lots 8 and 9 in the 5th concession, nor for lot 8 in the 4th concession.

NOTES
1. The Land Policies of Upper Canada.
2. Land Records, Nottawasaga, MS 658, Reel 348, Archives of Ontario.
3. #497 in above microfilm.
4. Archelaus Tupper, A Plan of Nottawasaga, a map.
5. #492 in above microfilm. There is an index of land records on microfiche which may be seen in Collingwood Library.
6. #489 in above microfilm.
7. #494, #495 in above microfilm. The land records index indicates the north

half of lot 9 in the 4th concession in the year 1842.

   8. #499 in above microfilm.

   9. #501 in above microfilm. There must have been some confusion here over this lot as it is recorded as well under #494 in 1843.

   10. #801 in above microfilm.

   11. #806 in above microfilm.

JOHN MCDONALD

It is not uncommon for people in this area to assume they are living on property once owned by our famous first prime minister, Sir John A. Macdonald. While going over the abstracts in the Land Registry Office in Barrie or otherwise searching the title of their property, sure enough, there will be the name John McDonald. A closer look, however, will indicate a difference in spelling. The man in question is the one who took over many of Archelaus Tupper's lots in the Tupper-Bowerman scheme of settlement after Tupper left the partnership. The story of the Tupper-Bowerman settlement may be found in Nottawasaga history books.

If he was not the first prime minister then just who was this man and what did he have to do with the development of Creemore? That will become clear as you read.

How did he qualify for these land grants? He was neither a war veteran nor a United Empire Loyalist. He was not a politician given favours for his particular stand on some matter. He did become a politician, but this was after he started acquiring the property. It appears that being a businessman at heart he applied for these grants when he saw the opportunity. It has been suggested that he was interested in the lots for his lumbering business,[1] but it was impossible at the time to transport timber from this area to Gananoque. It is even possible that he knew of the possibility of a railway line into the area.[2] Whatever the reason, he slowly acquired a number of lots.

Lots in Nottawasaga granted to John McDonald of Leeds County

lot 10, con. 5, 1837	lot 19, con. 7, 1842
lot 4, con. 5, 1837	lot 15, con. 7, 1842
lot 1, con. 4, 1837	lot 17, con. 7, 1842
lot 21, con. 7, 1837	lot 13, con. 7. 1842
lot 11, con. 7, 1840	lot 7, con. 12, 1842
lot 18, con. 7, 1840	lot 5, con. 12, 1842
lot 7, con. 4, 1841.	lot 19, con. 8, 1842
lot 11, con. 5, 1842	lot 3, con. 12, 1842
lot 17, con. 5, 1842	N1/2 lot 9, con. 4, 1842
lot 9, con. 6, 1842	lot 15, con. 5, 1842
lot 19, con. 4, 1842	lot 7, con. 5, 1842
lot 20, con. 4, 1842	lot 18, con. 4, 1842
lot 16, con. 6, 1842	lot 18, con. 8, 1844[3]
lot 10, con. 7, 1842	

John McDonald was a businessman, justice of the peace, office holder and politician. He was born February 10, 1787, in Saratoga, New York, the fourth son of John McDonald and Amelia Cameron. In 1831 he married Henrietta Maria Mallory and they had a family of one son and four daughters. McDonald died September 20, 1860 in Gananoque, Upper Canada.

John McDonald's brother, Charles, came to Gananoque in 1809, and during a visit by John in 1815 he may have been impressed by the success of his brother's business. In 1817, he joined his brother in partnership in there.

At the start the business was concerned primarily with lumbering to take advantage of the expanding British market. By 1825-27 the British were giving preferential treatment for Canadian wheat and flour and the firm quickly expanded their grist mill. This mill became the largest in Upper Canada and their flour, known as "Gananoque Mills" became famous.

John McDonald became justice of the peace in 1828 and also was appointed post master for Gananoque, a position which gave him free mailing privileges.

In 1839 McDonald received his first political appointment to the Legislative Council. During the Council's first session at Kingston, McDonald attended regularly but by 1843 his attendance was poor. In 1848 he had to give up his seat because of his frequent absences.

His large brick house built about 1831 is Gananoque Town Hall today.[4]

It is interesting to note, however, that Sir John A. Macdonald, before he was Prime Minister, held some land in Nottawasaga for a short time and sold it for a tidy profit. It was lot 12, concession 3.[5]

With all the lots McDonald had on his hands in Nottawasaga and a busy life in Gananoque, he had to make some business arrangement in order to profit from the grants. Now, it must be pointed out that it was not all clear profit. As a grant holder he had the responsibilities of bringing in settlers, preparing roads and getting mills built.

A young man by the name of William Nalty became his land agent.[6]

We don't know how he got his job as there seems to be no records any-where concerning it. He did live either in Gananoque or nearby.

And so, thanks to John McDonald and the man he hired, the birth of Creemore was in the works.

NOTES
1. The Gothic Rectory, p. 7.
2. A History of Simcoe County, p. 160.
3. Ontario Land Records, microfiche, Collingwood Library.
4. Dictionary of Canadian Biography, Vol. VIII, pp. 533-535.
5. Abstracts, Nottawasaga, Concession 3, Land Registry Office, Barrie.
6. William Nalty's name has been misspelled so often that it seems impossible to get it corrected. I have seen Nulty, McNulty, Naulty, Nalby, Naltee and Nally, all for one simple name. It is spelled Nalty in the Webster Family History, on his wife's tombstone and most convincingly of all, in his own signature. (Land Records, Nottawasaga, MS 658, Reel 348, #477, Ontario Archives.)

THE BEGINNINGS OF A VILLAGE

Was it 1842 or was it 1845? Maybe it was one of the years in between. The founding of our village, that is. The following account will help you make up your mind.

It was a long way from Gananoque to Nottawasaga Township in the early 1840s. William Nalty, a young man, displayed the courage of most early Ontario people by undertaking a journey of days that can now be accomplished in hours. He probably began his trip in a boat that plied its way along the north shore of Lake Ontario to Toronto. There he would take a stage or hitch a ride on a wagon to Holland Landing and from there he would travel on foot. According to the lore passed down to us he established a colonization office and a small government store containing settlers' effects at the corner of the Fourth Line and Sideroad 3-4 of Nottawasaga.[1] This, most likely, would be the north-west corner as this was one of the lots owned by John McDonald. Did he hire a man with a team of oxen to transport supplies? Did he build his little office and store by himself? Not likely, but who helped him? So many things we don't know.

When he came is an interesting point. It has been the accepted notion that he came in 1842. There are no documents or primary sources anywhere that tell us that but it is stated in <u>Nottawasaga: The Outburst of the Iroquois</u> that he came in that year.[2] Indeed, the date, 1842, is a reasonable one. McDonald amassed the most of his lots that year. A look through the certificates reveals that they were obtained over the course of the year.[3] It wouldn't be amiss to think that McDonald would send out young Nalty immediately to sell lots as quickly as possible.

Perhaps Nalty returned to his home in Leeds County in the fall. Not many prospective land owners would go land hunting in Nottawasaga's deep snow. This gave him a chance to start looking for a wife to share his life on the frontier. One, we know, caught his eye, for somewhere around 1845 he married Sarah Webster. In 1846 their daughter, also named Sarah, was born.[4] She appears to be the first child born in Creemore. The Nalty family did not remain in Creemore. In 1856, Sarah, William's wife, died and was buried in Oak Leaf Cemetery, Township of the Rear of Leeds and Lansdowne, Leeds County.[5] When daughter Sarah was married in 1875 she was living in Gananoque.

When William Nalty first arrived in Nottawasaga there were already a few people in the area, most particularly in the Lavender-Dunedin area, at Duntroon and on the Fourth Line north of Creemore. With new people choosing lots, growing grain and building homes it was important to construct some mills to make life easier. If a woman wanted flour to make bread someone had to hoist a bag of wheat over his/her shoulder and walk miles to Barrie, Hornings Mills or Adjala Township.

In 1835, Matthew Dowling along with his wife, came to lot 13, concession 5 on the Fourth Line just to the north of what is now Creemore.[6] They cleared land and built a cabin. In 1903, Mrs. Dowling recounted the story of her trip to Adjala to get some wheat ground into flour. Not only did she carry the sack of wheat but her baby daughter as well.[7] A grist mill on the Mad River would be welcomed by people such as Mrs. Dowling.

The settlers urged Nalty to build grist and saw mills, a plan which, no doubt, won the approval of John McDonald. Nalty, in turn, approached Edward Webster, the older brother of his girlfriend (unless he hadn't met Sarah until he began dealing with Edward). Edward Webster agreed to come. Now we don't know to what extend he was supported by McDonald. Building a mill doesn't come cheaply and Edward Webster was by no means a rich man. Perhaps money was advanced. Perhaps free land was the enticement. A young man, born in the forests of Leeds County, knew how to cope with pioneer conditions, and probably had dreams of success given this opportunity.

The story of his trip to Creemore has been published many times. Almost certainly this account was written by Frank Webster, Edward's nephew, the only one around with a link to the past, at the time it was written.

"Mr. Edward Webster...the following year [1843] loaded a saw outfit, a run of stones and a carding mill on a boat at Brockville and sailed around the lakes, arriving at the mouth of the Nottawasaga River. From there he had the outfit conveyed across to Creemore. Mr. Joe Slack, better known as Quaker Joe (a mill wright), was engaged to construct this mill and fit the machinery into it.

By March, 1844, a mill was built, 24' x 60', situated on the flats between the present old mill dam and the river. They now started to cut lumber with an old sash saw driven by a flutter water wheel. In the meantime Mr. McNulty's [should be Nalty] office and store were moved to Creemore to a new building. This building is still standing. It is the kitchen of Mr. John Aikens' house. [John Wiggins lives there now.] In 1845 a run of stones was put in the east end of the mill which ground the grain as the farmers carried it on their backs or on an ox sled. There was no smutter on this mill and of course the flour was often dirty and black. Even this was better than packing wheat long distances to be made into flour.

In 1850 a lean-to 12' wide was built on the east end of the mill, where the first carding machine in the township was installed and operated. In 1847 George Webster (brother of Edward Webster) arrived and operated this combination mill until the new flour mill was built in 1853."[8]

The mill terminology may be unfamiliar to you. Some investigation produced the following results. The flutter wheel was a rather primitive and inefficient water wheel with not much power. It was the kind you might see operating now for ornamental purposes. There is one at the side of the road at Glen Huron. The sash saw suited this type of water wheel as a circular saw would require more power. It was set in a frame and ran up and down and sawed the logs into rough lumber. The smutter for flour was, as you might imagine, some sort of sieve to remove the coarseness from the flour and perhaps the smut, which is a disease. A carder is for smoothing out the fibres of sheeps' wool. There are hand carders but a carding mill would speed up the process and assist the women who worked hard enough as it was.

In the quotation about the mill is the name, Quaker Joe Slack, the mill wright who supervised the building of the mill. A clipping from the Brockville Recorder and Times tells of the discovery of some of Joseph Slack's letters. "Mrs. C.E. Johnston, of Brockville, who is the former Rachel Boyce, of Athens, has revealed several letters written by her grandfather, Joseph Slack, an Empire Loyalist, the first mill wright to settle north of Brockville in Leeds County...The letters, mailed without the use of envelopes, are still quite well preserved. They tell of the trials of the early pioneer workman, often separated from his wife and family for many months while engaged in constructing a mill at Perth, Ont., or some other location which in those days was a long way from home. They tell also of the heartache and loneliness which was often-times the lot of both man and wife. Mr. and Mrs. Slack, the early pioneers were also devout Quakers."[9]

Numerous letters of inquiry have been written concerning Quaker Joe and his letters but have brought little success. As the newspaper report referred to had no date it was difficult to know how old it was. Finally someone was found who knew about the letters. Reading them would be the earliest first person account of life in Creemore. But it was not to be. The letters were donated to the Ontario Archives in Toronto and have been lost there. The staff have conducted at least two searches but the letters have not been found.

What date can we pin to Creemore's founding? A large portrait commissioned by Edward Webster, himself, and given to his brother, George, has the most convincing bit of proof. Inscribed during the photographic process are the words, "Edward Webster, The Founder of the Village of Creemore, 1845." [10]

NOTES
1. Nottawasaga: The Outburst of the Iroquois, p. 105.
2. See above.
3. Nottawasaga Land Records, Archives of Ontario, MS 658, Reel 348.
4. Ontario Marriage Registrations, MS 932, Reel 17, p. 212. Sarah's birthdate can be deduced from her marriage registration as it gives her age and the date of marriage.
5. Oak Leaf Cemetery Index, page 8.
6. The Dowling Family History, p. 2.
7. Creemore Star, May 14, 1903.
8. Nottawasaga: The Outburst of the Iroquois, p. 105.
9. News and Views, Leeds and Grenville Branch of the Ontario Genealogical Society, April-May, 1995, p. 45.
10. This portrait is now in the hands of Helen Emmett Blackburn.

A NAME AND A POST OFFICE

How DID we get our name? Two accounts of Creemore's naming have been around for years. One states that Creemore was named after the Cree Indians. This is quite false with no substance to it. The Crees were not in this area or anywhere near. The second account tells us that the name had a Scottish origin.[1] This is not correct either. The name has an Irish origin.

The honour of naming the village goes to Judge J. R. Gowan, a native of Ireland. The word is from the Gaelic, "cree mohr", meaning "big heart." Creemore is also the name of a townland in County Wexford, Ireland.

In 1958 the author had the privilege of visiting the Webster home-stead, Garrybritt, near Enniscorthy, County Wexford. While there, in conversation with Webster relatives, she brought up the name of Creemore. The Garrybritt Websters indicated that a country area nearby was called Creemore. This matter came up again during another visit to Ireland in 1993. Determined to find Creemore, your author and her husband drove to the approximate area, checked in a farm supply store for the exact location and was told it was just down the road and to the left. There it was! Creemore! The road through it was shaded by trees and all that could be seen was a hay field and a house in the distance. Creemore is not a village but a townland. Townlands in Ireland are areas of various sizes without municipal governments. They were formed many, many years ago, their boundaries seemingly decided by sheep or cattle as they trod paths through the fields. They may range in size from three acres to several hundred. A couple of people who understood Gaelic were asked what Creemore meant, and, sure enough, they confirmed that it meant "big heart." Creemore may be found today on any map of Wexford that shows the townlands.

James Gowan, who named the village, spent his youth in this part of Ireland and would have known the name, Creemore. It is possible he visited the townland and liked it. A search of property owners and tenants in that time frame did not indicate any likely relatives.[2] The home of Edward Webster's father was about five miles distant from Creemore and a bit further from James Gowan's home. Perhaps Edward and the Judge collaborated, thinking fondly of their homeland. Perhaps the Judge was treated kindly in Creemore and thought the name appropriate. All of this, of course, is pure conjecture. A search through his papers, both at the Simcoe County Archives, Midhurst, and the Ontario Archives, Toronto, resulted not in the smallest clue regarding the naming of Creemore.

There are two dates for the establishment of the first post office in Creemore. The same book that tells us the name, Creemore, was Scottish, also tells us that the first post office was established in 1854. Two other sources say the post office was opened in 1849.[3] "Which is correct?" There was only one way to be sure, and that was to check the official records at the National Archives in Ottawa. This was quickly researched. The first post office was opened August 6, 1851. The name was Creemore Mills and the first post master was E. Webster. So, it was neither 1849 or 1854 but another year altogether. However, it is possible that an unofficial post office had been set up in 1849 with a volunteer moving the mail between Creemore and Duntroon, the nearest official post office.

From an interview conducted in 1907, we may learn of the mail delivery system in the pioneer days. The interview was with James More of Dunedin.[4] "During the late forties a Mr. Hunter, who lived on the Penetang road, had the contract to carry the mail from Barrie to Owen Sound. Owing to ill health he re-let the contract to Mr. More's father. James was then about 18 years old, and used to carry the mail for all the country between Barrie and Owen Sound and ride on horseback in summer. In winter he used a sleigh. He wore thick boots and warm clothes but never an overcoat or overshoes, and never was frozen except the tip of his nose...

The mail route started at Barrie, where the post office was kept by Mr. Sanford. The next office was at Sunnidale Corners kept by Mr. Gillespie. Where Stayner stands was then a howling wilderness, and he followed a rough bush road through what is now the main street, directly west to Duntroon, where the office was kept by Mr. McNabb." The terminus was the general store in Owen Sound. The trip was made every week.

NOTES
1. The Origin of the Names of the Post Offices of Simcoe County, p. 19.
2. Griffith's Valuation. This assessment was done in Ireland in the mid 1800s and may be seen on microfiche in the Toronto Reference Library, near the corner of Yonge and Bloor Streets.
3. Nottawasaga: The Outburst of the Iroquois, p. 106, and A History of Simcoe County, p. 244.
4. Nottawasaga: The Outburst of the Iroquois, p. 42.

JUDGE JAMES R. GOWAN

Now that we know Creemore was named by Judge James R. Gowan, a prominent man, the next thing , it seems, is to learn his story.

The name of Gowan has been prominent in Creemore for many years so it will be helpful to investigate the relationship between the Judge and the Creemore Gowans. The relationship is distant and makes it necessary to go back to 1700 to find a common ancestor.[1] James Gowan's family were from Wexford, Ireland, and the Creemore Gowans came from Queens County, now called Laois [pronounced Leesh]. However, the common Irish background and the name are a bond.

James Gowan wrote an account of his life which appears in <u>The Genealogy of the Clan Gowan</u>.[2] Here in his own words are his memories of his youth. "My father tried a good many things with doubtful advantage and I can recollect enough to know that farming in which he engaged for some time could not have been very profitable. He decided to sell all he had and seek a new home in Canada, which he did, sailing in 1832 in 'The Horsely Hill', from New Ross, a party of six, my mother and two sisters, myself, and one servant. The vessel was only 800 tons and, though we had a cabin to ourselves, it was not very comfortable I can remember. We had over 300 steerage passengers on board. First and last we were four months from the time we started until we landed in Quebec, for we were dismasted about one thousand miles from land, driven back under 'jury masts', fortunately to Waterford for my Uncle, Dr. James Burkitt, resided there. We remained in his house till the vessel was refitted and ready for sea.

We reached Quebec in the Fall, proceeding directly from there to Little York, now Toronto. My father ultimately purchased in the township of Albion about twenty-five miles from Toronto, two very nice farms. They were only ordinary farm buildings but my father and I went out and he soon had a nice, large, comfortable residence erected, more land cleared and everything brought into good order.

After about a year on the farm, I was brought to Toronto and articled to the Hon. James Edward Small, Solicitor General under the Baldwin-La Fontaine Administration, my father arranging that I should live with him and paying him a small fee of 360 [Pounds] for five years.

I completed my articles in 1838 and the day following he offered me, and I accepted, a partnership with him on terms of half profits but then almost the whole work of the office was left to me, for Mr. Small was immersed in politics. In August 1839 I was called to the Bar. From that time I took nearly all the business, and it was heavy. I am safe in saying that I worked on the average fourteen hours of every twenty-four and without holidays, for a period of nearly four years, frequently on Sundays, I am sorry to say. My health was completely broken down and my medical man, Dr. Kong, said to me: 'You will be in a lunatic asylum or the grave in six months, if you continue to work as you do.' In the course of my professional duties I frequently came in contact with the Hon. Robert Baldwin, the Premier of Canada, who spontaneously offered me the post of Judge in the newly formed Judicial District of Simcoe, the largest in Canada. I accepted, knowing the duties would give me a good deal of horseback riding exercise, the very thing I required. I went to Barrie in 1843. My acceptance involved a serious loss of income."

Although an account of his life in Barrie makes one doubt whether it was less stressful than his work in Toronto, his health did return. The area he took over was the largest in the province and included 30 townships, taking in the area from the eastern shores of Lake Huron, easterly to Lake Simcoe and north to include Muskoka and Parry Sound.[3] Some of his court cases were 100 miles apart. He went to the people. The people did not travel long distances to a Barrie courthouse. On one occasion he found himself at dark far from a house that could give him shelter for the night. He upturned his sleigh for shelter from the wind and spent the night wrapped in his buffalo robe.

On that occasion he had a sleigh but at other times, due to the poor conditions of the trails he had to use a saddle horse or his own sturdy legs. On one of his trips from Barrie to Collingwood the forest was on fire . The smoke and heat were bad enough, but there was also considerable peril from the burning trees falling around him.

The court sittings were in the various crude buildings available in the pioneer communities, often the local taverns. At one trial the crowd was so large it was necessary to hold the sitting in the open air, but "he was able, by virtue of his presence, to import into such unusual surroundings, all the dignity and decorum of a Court of Law."

Gowan took his position seriously and worked hard. He won the people's respect and admiration and was revered by his profession. He was "appealed to by settlers for advice in their local and family affairs, and many differences, which might have become open feuds, [which] were happily settled by his wise counsel."

He was a member of the Reformed Episcopal Church in Barrie and took a prominent part in its affairs. However, he was also a liberal supporter of other religions. He donated a manse and large plot of land to the Presbyterians and a 100 acre improved farm near Minesing, in trust for Wesleyan and Primitive Methodists and Baptists. He also took responsibility in his community in the field of education and was for many years a school trustee.

A 1978 review of his life appeared in a Barrie newspaper.[4] From it we may learn of his many accomplishments and honours outside of his career as a Judge in Simcoe County. He served on some important Commissions, one being to investigate the Pacific Scandal of 1873. He worked for Sir John A. Macdonald in the preparations of his legal forms, working with him some time before each session engaged in the preparations of measures for the improvement of the law and its administration.

On a trip to England he had conferred upon him the honourary degree of LLD at the University of Queen's College. In Canada he was appointed to the Senate.

As you drive through Barrie you will see a Gowan Street named after him. As well, there is an Ardagh Road named after his wife's family. When you see these names you can give a thought to the man who cared so much about our early pioneers, brought justice to the hinterlands, and named our little village.

NOTE
1. Genealogy of the Clan Gowan.
2. See above, pp. 268, 269.
3. His life as a Judge is taken from Life of Sir James Gowan 1815-1909, pp. 6, 9, 16-18,170, 176,181.
4. The Examiner, Barrie, April 28, 1978, p. 29.

CREEMORE IN 1853

There comes a moment in every researcher's life that is truly exciting. The discovery of the 1853 map of Creemore in the Ontario Archives is a good example.[1] It gives a picture of Creemore which has hitherto been unavailable for such an early date in history.

There are no other primary records for this time period. Unfortunately the 1851 Census for all of Simcoe County went missing some time before that year was microfilmed. While other areas can get a snapshot of their area at that time, we can't. There are no assessment records for that period either.

The map is labeled, "Creemore, The Property of Edward Webster, Laid Out for the Proprietor into quarter and half acre lots, by William Gibbard, Dec., 1853." We may assume that Gibbard did the surveying in the warmer months of 1853 and finished preparing the map by December. It is a large map and if it were to be reproduced for this book the print would be impossible to read. For that reason there is a drawing of the area where most of the activity took place and notes about the rest.

In the upper corner of the map is the following message: "This property is situated in the midst of a thickly settled agricultural country, not surpassed for raising Wheat in Canada, at the intersection of 6 leading lines of Road as follows:- To the East to the proposed Central Station of the Northern Rail Road at Coates' Creek, a distance of 6 miles. West to Ospry, [sic] Proton, Melancthon and Artemesia the shortest and best line for the inhabitants of 25 square miles of well settled agricultural Country to reach the Northern Rail Road. South East-the Mail line to Barrie. Northerly-the Mail line to Collingwood Euphrasia St Vincent and Owen Sound. Southerly-the line to West Essa Cookstown Bond Head & Bradford and South Westerly-the line to Mulmur Tosorontio, Mono & Adjala.

All these lines are travelled and can be seen on Gibbard's Map of the County. The Water Privilege on Mad river is too well known to need comment. Pine of the best quality in abundance within 2 miles.

The proprietor has been hitherto deterred from making improvements from the utter impossibility of getting in or out with a load for 9 months in the year, the Northern Rail Road within 6 miles has now already induced the Proprietor to go ahead & make extensive improvements & a better opening can seldom be met with for all kinds of Mechanics."

Starting at the south, about where the cemetery entrance of today may be found is Napier Street running to the west. This is followed by Anne, Edward, Elizabeth and Caroline Streets. They all run to the west, and, of course, the only one we have now is Caroline running westward through the country. On the north side of the river are George, Edward, Elizabeth, Caroline, Francis, Wellington and Louisa Streets. The north-south streets, starting way west of the Caroline Street bridge were William, Alice, Sarah, Collingwood, Mill, Jane, Mary, Robert and John. Francis Street, after it crossed Collingwood Street ran at a north-west angle to meet Louisa Street.

Edward named most of these streets after his family. His wife was Elizabeth Ann, his daughters were Elizabeth and Caroline; and his sons, Francis and Wellington. Edward is himself. William and Alice were his parents. George, Robert and John were his brothers and Sarah and Jane were his sisters.

The small drawing of the area south of the river shows a pioneer industrial park. [See illustrations] In one small area are all the services needed for survival. The mill races show an ingenious design for making use of the water power. Each of the mill races would require a bridge, as well as the ones over the river at Caroline, Collingwood and Mill Streets. Everything was accessible.

With the very few houses in what was to become a village, it is hard to imagine there would be enough people for the church and enough children for the school. However, there were many farmers in the surrounding hills so that the school and the church could be filled.

The year 1853 was both a good year and a very difficult year for Edward Webster. Full of optimism with news of the railroad coming to within a short distance of Creemore he could see a rosy and prosperous future selling lots, bringing people to the village and his businesses growing because of it. He had been married in 1847 in Eastern Ontario to Elizabeth Ann Tremayne, the daughter of a well known Church of England minister. They had four children, Francis, Elizabeth, Caroline and Wellington. As it often happened in those days Elizabeth Ann died a few days after the birth of Wellington in January, of 1853. She was among the first burials in the cemetery. Her stone is a white slab near some lilacs by the top of the steep bank that overlooked her old home.

Edward persevered, however, and the little settlement continued to grow. He remained active in the community and was involved in the operation of both the school and the church. In 1853 he arranged for the building of a new grist and flour mill to replace what had been set up in the first mill.

The following information about Creemore in the 1850s and 60s is from Nottawasaga: The Outburst of the Iroquois.[2]

One curious bit of information that has been in the local histories for at least 70 years is that Andrew Giffen settled on the west half of lot 9, con. 4. He paid $300 for the farm and cleared most of the land and sold it to Edward Webster in 1864 for $800. Giffen's name, however, is not in the abstract for lot 9, concession 4, or for any other property in Creemore. Also, Edward Webster had left Creemore in 1864. There must be some truth somewhere about this. We could conjecture that the transaction was not recorded in the Registry Office or that Andrew Giffen rented the property and over the years the story got confused.

Mr. Giffen's family born at Creemore were John, James and Elizabeth. James, when a small boy, drowned in the river at the Fourth Line bridge.

"A Mr. Trout, a well known mill wright, with his sons constructed the new mill. In the raising of this mill one of the men got his leg broken. A Mr. Sanderson, living north of Creemore on the fourth line, who was a handy man at any job, was sent for. He set the leg, and a doctor was sent for. When the doctor arrived he pronounced Mr. Sanderson's job as properly done...[In 1854] George Webster constructed the first frame tavern in Creemore for Sam Wilcox on George Street... The first tavern in Creemore was a log building situated...on Mill Street at the turn of the street. [This appears to be the one on the 1853 map labeled Creemore Inn] Mr. Christy Connor kept this tavern. No licence was required at this time. This was not a paying proposition so he deserted the business and moved to a farm on lot 21, concession 7. This tavern was pulled down and a new tavern was built in its place by George Webster, for William Gowan in 1859. In 1855 George Webster built a second tavern for Wm. Kelly situated on the south west corner of Mill and Edward Streets...In

1860 he built a store on the north east corner of Mill and Edward Streets for Mr. Geo. Bolster. Previous to this Mr. Bolster kept store south of the river on Mill Street. William Thornbury kept store in this new store after Bolster moved to Orillia.

Mr. George Evans was the first blacksmith in Creemore. His shop stood on the 4th line between the mill dam and the river on the east side of the road. [See map.] William Casey at a later date started a blacksmith and wagon making shop on Edward Street. [See map.] Robert Steele started a blacksmith shop at the south end of Mill Street. Mr. Henry Mathers ran a wagon making shop close to Mr. Steele's shop.

About 1864 a young man by the name of Rueben Smith, who belonged to a well known family on lot 16, con. 6, started to do business in Creemore. He was a man of great energy, and probably one of the most enterprising, and at the same time, reckless plungers that ever did business in Creemore. He opened a store in the building that is now the Rinn house.[3] He just nicely got started in this store when he built a woolen mill on Edward Street opposite the Orange Hall...He just operated this mill two years when he built a much larger woolen mill driven by water power west of the bridge on Caroline Street. The first woolen mill went out of use. He built a store in Dunedin and put his brother, William, in charge of it. This all happened within ten years. The inevitable happened. The business crashed."

NOTES
1. Creemore: The Property of Edward Webster, 1853 map.
2. Nottawasaga: The Outburst of the Iroquois, pp 104-107.
3. A note by Alice Emmett indicates that this was once the Bob Barber house. It is now the John and Evelyn Knappett house.

ONTARIO, HURON AND SIMCOE RAILWAY

It is a surprising fact that there was a way to get to Toronto from Collingwood in the earliest pioneer days at about the same speed that it takes for a form of public transportation in 1999. Read on.

Probably the most significant event in the years 1832-1871 was the building of the railroad from Toronto to Barrie to Collingwood, the latter which was then known as Hen and Chickens. The first engine arrived at Hen and Chickens December 14, 1854, and a passenger train three weeks later.[1] Not only did the train ease the passage of settlers and their belongings into the area, but it brought prosperity, particularly with the squared timber trade. While this line did not pass through Creemore, the eight miles to Stayner and six to New Lowell made it close enough to enjoy its benefits. Although there were at least two short railways prior to the building of the Toronto-Barrie-Collingwood line, this one is considered the first major railroad in Canada. Please note that although the route is described as through Barrie, it actually was to Allandale a mile or two from Barrie. Allandale is now amalgamated with the city of Barrie.

Attempts were made to establish this railroad in 1836 and 1845 by acts in the Canadian Legislature, but it wasn't until the 1849 act that the chartering company succeeded in their task.[2] In 1850 it received its name, the Ontario, Simcoe and Huron Railway, which became known locally as Oats, Straw and Hay.

But, then, what fuss, furore and agitation! There were those that doubted if it could be built. "I hope the people won't consider you crazy," wrote one man in a letter to the editor in Barrie.[3] As usual, when major projects such as this are presented there was great consternation about the increase in local taxes. Simcoe County had to raise 50,000 Pounds in debentures payable in 20 years.[4] Such was the commotion that an area on the south side of the Holland River left the County and several townships separated to form Grey County.[5] The financial concerns were not easily solved, but finally the smoke cleared and the railroad came into existence.

The early steam engines operated on good hard wood of which there was an abundance along the line. The engine did not carry sufficient fuel for the entire trip. Every so often four blasts of the whistle were sounded which brought to their feet a crew of men at the next woodpile. When the engine stopped they quickly sprang into action and loaded up enough wood for the next few miles. This was called "wood-up."[6]

Some of the early engines on the route were the Lady Elgin, the Josephine,[7] the Collingwood, the Simcoe and the Toronto.[8] One of their features was a very large smoke stack which had a screen over the opening to trap the worst of the still burning embers and soot. The arrival of these noisy, smoke-belching monsters into the wilderness must have been a sight to behold. Up to this time slow, plodding oxen or perhaps a saddle horse were the only examples of moving power greater than man.

Another feature on the engine was the cow catcher. The designers of the engine were sure that any roving cow would be swept up with the catcher and tossed into the ditch. It didn't work and a cow caused the first Canadian train wreck. When she was struck by the engine two of the cars went over her but the third car went rolling down the ditch. The car was a total loss.[9] No mention was made of the total loss of the cow.

Not everyone could make use of the train. The economy operated mainly on the barter system and cash was what was needed for train fare or for shipping goods. If a person had cash consider how easy it was to get to Toronto. Just ten years previously it was necessary to walk from Creemore to Holland Landing, most likely with a pack on one's back. In the heady days of the first train rides to Toronto it was necessary only to walk to New Lowell (then called Sunnidale) or Stayner (Nottawasaga) to catch the train there. It might have taken only three hours to get to Toronto on the train.[10] County officers, Members of Parliament and church dignitaries made great use of this means of travel to conduct their business.[11] Four trains a day plied the line and in one year brought in $100,000.[12] Conductors were picked for their gentlemanliness and sobriety making each trip a pleasant affair. A train ride had a touch of glamour and class hitherto unknown in this area. No wonder it was so popular.

A real coup for this area and the Ontario, Simcoe and Huron Railway occurred in September, 1860.[13] His Royal Highness, Albert, Prince of Wales, came to this country and went for a ride on the train. The whole country was in a fever pitch and, no doubt, people from the Creemore area made the trip to Collingwood or the Sunnidale and Nottawasaga stations to catch a glimpse of royalty. Collingwood, just five years old at the time, and quite small, attracted 10,000 people.[14]

An observation car was built for the occasion. It was essentially a small flat car with a railing but was fitted out with carpet and upholstered seats. The Prince, dressed in a white hat, blue coat and grey trousers remained on the observation car for almost the entire trip.[15]

Those who couldn't make the long trip to Collingwood gathered at Sunnidale and Nottawasaga stations where tall arches of evergreens were placed over the track. At Nottawasaga Station even bagpipes were playing as the train went past the station. Fortunately the engine wasn't capable of any great speed as the timetable indicated that the train would slow down at Angus but not at Sunnidale or Nottawasaga.[16]

An amusing story has been told by Ross Fraser of Banda. He heard it from a man from Sunnidale who was helping in the construction of a barn at the Fraser farm. It concerns a man from Sunnidale Township who went to see the Prince of Wales, probably in Collingwood. He was anxious to get a piece of Crown Land that was near his property, perhaps for a pasture farm. This fellow was able to get near enough the Royal Prince to make him hear. He said, "Say, Prince, did you ever hear your mother say what she was going to do with that piece of land she owns in Sunnidale Township?"

The excitement of that day soon passed although its memory probably warmed the hearts of those early citizens through many a long, cold winter. A train that brought royalty to Creemore's doorstep, however, was a minor occurrence compared to the economic boom which soon developed.

Until the arrival of the railroad farmers sustained their families but had no market for their farm products. Suddenly, a trip to Stayner or New Lowell, admittedly time consuming and often uncomfortable, meant that goods could be shipped to a ready market in Toronto.

The largest development was in the timber trade. The huge pines and other trees that stood in the way of clearing the land now became valuable. In 1861, the timber trains started running to Toronto January 7th and went constantly until the 31st of August.[17] That was a lot of timber. It could then be used there or shipped to England or other parts of the world. The Pine Plains south of Angus had a spur line with cars drawn by horses.[18]

The spin-off for all this activity most certainly would be of benefit to Creemore. Young men would find work. More families would move to the area, more stores would be needed, more craftsmen and servicemen could find work, more farmers would find markets for their produce and a spirit of optimism would prevail for the future success of the area.

NOTE
1. Four Whistles to Wood-Up: Stories of the Northern Railway of Canada, p. 42.
   2. The History of Simcoe County, p. 160.
   3. See above, p. 162.
   4. See above, p. 164.
   5. See above. p. 165.
   6. Four Whistles to Wood-Up, p. 5.
   7. See above, p. 37.
   8. The History of Simcoe County, p. 169.
   9. Four Whistles to Wood -Up, pp. 31-32.
   10. In a letter written by W. Sanders, July 8, 1855, he says, "You can go from Toronto to Collingwood now in three hours!" From an article, "A Letter from Penetanguishene," Ontario History, Vol.XL, Toronto, 1948.
   11. Four Whistles to Wood-Up, p. 53.
   12. See above, p. 53.
   13. See above, p. 8.
   14. See above, p. 52.
   15. See above, p. 51.
   16. See above, p. 8.
   17. See above, p. 55.
   18. See above, p. 55.

THE CANADIAN DIRECTORY FOR 1857-58[1]

Directories are a great help in looking at pictures of the past. There are city directories where everyone is listed, county directories, provincial directories and there is even one that lists places in all of Canada and the United States. An agent would come into a town and canvass the people to get the information. They can't be counted on to be completely accurate as people could be missed or unwilling to give details.

Creemore Mills, C. W.[3] A flourishing village situated on the Mad river in the Township of Nottawasaga, and County of Simcoe. There is a large business done in lumber and flour. Distant from Sunnidale Station, 6 miles, from Nottawasaga Station, 8 miles, and from Collingwood Harbour, 15 miles. Mail, tri weekly. Population about 200.

Bolster, George J., storekeeper
Campbell, Alexander, tanner
Casey, William, blacksmith
Galloway, H., carpenter
Hammond & Co., saw mill
Hill, Edward, school teacher
Hogg, William, boot and shoemaker
Kelly, William, tavernkeeper
Kendrick, John, carpenter and builder
Langtry, Rev. John, B.A., Church of England
Martin, John., Carpenter and builder
Moore, Robert, cooper
Siddle, H., waggonmaker
Thornbury, F. C., storekeeper
Webster, Edward, postmaster and proprietor of saw and flour mills
Webster, George, carding and fuller mills
Wilcox, Samuel, tavernkeeper

NOTES
  1. The Canadian Directory for 1857-58.
  2. Stands for Canada West.

1858 ASSESSMENT

Included in this book are assessment records and census reports. There is no analysis of this information. You might like to do so yourself. There are several things you might like to look at: the names, the occupations of the time, the youthful ages of the people in business, the streets that had the most people, the religions, the ethnic origins. Some details are in the assessments and some in the census reports. If you look closely you will also see that there must be inaccuracies. For example, the ages don't add up from one year to another. All the information in the assessments, is not included, for example, the value of the property.

Name	Occupation	Age	Property
William Casey	Blacksmith	26	N. Edward St. 11 & 12
			S. Elizabeth St. 11 & 12
Edward Webster	Gentleman	4	N1/2 7
		4	Pt. 8
		4	S.W Pt. 9
		5	Pt. E.1/2 8
		5	S.W. Pt. 9
			S. Edward St. 11 & 12
James Langtry Sen.	Carpenters	50, 25	E. Coll'd St. Letter A
Wm, James & John Langtry		22, 21	
Patrick Delany	Yeoman	35	N. Edward St. 62
Leonard Nulty	Stage Driver	25	S. Caroline St. 41, 42
William E. Walker	Miller	25	W. Mill St. Letter C
George J. Bolster	Merchant	26	N. Edward St. 13, 18, 19
			S. Edward St. 21, 22, 23, 24
James Hudson	Yeoman	26	S. Edward St. 13, 14
			N. Edward St. 20, 21, 22
Samuel Wilcox	Inn Keeper	31	George St. 2, 3
Stephan Lyman	Preacher	38	N. Caroline St. 51
George Webster	Yeoman	30	S. Edward St. 9
			Con. 5 W1/2 10
			Con. 5 Pt. S.W. 1/4 9
Henry Siddall	Wagon Maker	28	N. Elizabeth St. 12
			W. Mill St. ??
Wm H. Thornbury	Merchant	20	N.W. corner Edward and Mill Street 12

Name	Occupation	Age	Property
John Hogg & Executors of the Estate			Corner of Elizabeth
Wm H. Thornbury	Of the late Wm Hogg		& Collingwood St 42
Nicholas Hogg	Wagon Maker	26	N. Elizabeth Street 43
John G. Martin	Carpenter	26	S. Edward Street 17
			N. George St. &
			E. Mill Street 4 & 5

FIGHTING AND FUN AT THE FAIR

What people now refer to as Collingwood Fair or The Great Northern Exhibition once held its events in different spots around the township. Even its earliest fairs were great successes as the following account indicates. Following that is a report of the third fair held in Creemore in 1858. It was written by Frank Webster and appeared in the Creemore Star, July 27, 1994. Mr. Webster always loved a good story but you will see he reveals his habit of self-righteous moralizing.

REPORT OF THE 1860 NOTTAWASAGA
AGRICULTURAL SOCIETY[1]

The Directors of the Nottawasaga Branch Agricultural Society, beg to leave report that the Society this year consists of 115 members which is a great increase in the number reported for 1859, and which evidently exhibits more interest in Agricultural affairs and a desire to promote competition and produce improvement in the various branches of that science. The sum subscribed during the year amounts to $160.50. The Legislative Grant to $63.33 and the balance from 1859, $42.79, making total receipts $266.62. The amount paid in premiums at the annual exhibition and ploughing match was $185.50. The expenses during the year amounted to $48.16, leaving a balance in the hands of the Treasurer of $32.96. The Society held the fifth annual exhibition of Grain, Stock, Implements of Husbandry &c., on the 3rd of October last, at Bowmore[2] there was a greater display of Horses, Cattle, and articles for competition than had been on any previous occasion of the kind, and more desire was evident on the part of the various competitors to excel in what was brought forward.

The specimens of grain were excellent, and it seemed to be the general impression upon the minds of the people that it was the most successful exhibition since the formation of the Society.

The ploughing match took place on the 5th of October following, on the farm of A. Jardine, Esq. The competition was very keen, and the work done beautiful, and was spoken of by the Judges in the highest terms of commendation.

We consider that it would be an omission if we did not take notice of the support given to the Society by J.D. Stephens, Esq., at the ploughing match, by his liberal premiums to the young ploughmen, and also by his continuing to import into the Township, improved breeds of Stock.

It also gives us much pleasure to state that the entire horses which travelled the Township have been of a superior description, and more suitable for raising stock for farm purposes.

We would also mention an improvement generally adopted throughout the Township, by the farmers ploughing up old meadows for a succession of crops, which had hitherto lain for many years under hay, which yielded an unprofitable return, and in many cases would make very poor pasture.

We would also say that the crops have been most abundant and yielded well particularly Fall and Spring Wheat which is the staple crop of this Township. We would, however, say to the farmers of Nottawasaga not to rest satisfied, but to make fresh advances in the cultivation and management of their farms, and they will in due time reap the benefit of doing so. The clearing of new land has also progressively advanced, and a larger amount of Fall Wheat has been sown upon it than was hitherto in one year, the soil being favourable to the production of that kind of grain.

Much good is expected to result from the circumstance, that a considerable portion of the wild lands in this Township held by speculators, has during the year, passed into the hands of practical farmers. We hope to see a continuation of these changes.

THE FAIR IN CREEMORE IN 1858

How many years have passed since the Township of Nottawasaga had an agricultural society? In conversation with John Davis I learned it was organized many years before I was born.

The first fair was held at Duntroon, the second one at Stayner, and the third one in Creemore in September 1858. The amusements, the joys, the social conditions of the people and their shortcomings as told by our old men give us a picture of the life of our forefathers which we all find interesting.

At this date the present generation may read these stories with some surprise and may conclude they belong to a higher civilization. Nevertheless let it be remembered that old times possessed a hospitality and a kindly spirit of co-operation that is hard to find in our present generation.

At that date there was no such thing as "doles" provided by the governments. The people of those days possessed the courage and the resourcefulness to provide for themselves and "were too proud" for someone else to keep them. These men and women were willing to live within their incomes and they had at all times kind neighbours to help them in the production of food for their families. What a pity that more of that spirit is not with us today.

Let us go back to this Agricultural Fair in Creemore. It was held on the common between Elizabeth and Caroline Streets and Mill and Collingwood Streets. One of the largest crowds Mr. Davis ever saw at Creemore attended that fair. He estimated that there were three thousand present. They came from Duntroon, Stayner, Collingwood, New Lowell, Glencairn, Mulmur Township, Maple Valley, and Singhampton.

Entries for farm products were many and the competition between exhibitors was keen. The wagon makers exhibited their wagons and the blacksmiths their handiwork. Some implements were also shown. Ten splendid teams of horses were lined up for first money. Mr. Alex McArthur got first place for a fine team.

While the fair was a great success it was also a time when whiskey flowed freely. About every thirty feet in distance, drunks could be seen with their coats off wanting to fight using language that would not sound proper at a prayer meeting.

However, Mr. Davis said there were always some accommodating enough to hold them back so that nothing serious resulted. When evening came a dance was held at Alex Sutherland's tavern which Mr. Davis attended. While the dancing was going on the usual crowd was at the bar swallowing up booze and talking about fighting. Towards midnight Mr. Davis and his friends decided to go home but dropped into Kelly's tavern on their way. There they counted about thirty men so drunk they were lying on the floor, although talking of fighting they couldn't do so on account of their condition.

NOTES

1. <u>Northern Advance</u>, Barrie, Ontario, 23 Jan., 1861, p. 2, c. 5. May be seen on microfilm at the Simcoe County Archives, Midhurst.

2. Now Duntroon.

1861 MAP[1]

By 1861 Creemore was getting bigger and better. With bright hopes for the future Edward Webster had a new survey done for Creemore by W. Sanders and a new map made.

This particular map, is registered in the Registry Office, Barrie, as official plan #88. An original copy was available in Creemore but it is missing. Another original copy has been carefully preserved by a great great nephew of Edward Webster, Donald Webster. On it are hand drawn sketches of several buildings which have been reproduced for this book. As the hand printing on both the 1853 map and the 1861 one are the same, it appears that Edward Webster made the sketches.

This 1861 map indicates how much Creemore has grown in the time period after the 1853 map was made. There are more streets and more buildings and more surveyed lots ready for the prospective purchaser.

Ambitious plans were in the making for the south side of the river. Gone was the industrial park on the flat beside the river. Only the house and barn of Mr. Webster, two grist mills and the old store remained. In place of the other buildings and one of the mill races were more streets and lots.

On the south side of the river and east of the Fourth Line were Herbert, Webster, Nalty, Napier, Peel, Kate, Church and Mountain Streets. Still on the south side of the river but west of the fourth line were Tremayne, Ann, a continuation of Webster, Alice, William, Laura and Water Streets. On the north side Nelson and Langtry Streets were added but John and Robert Streets to the east were left out.

With the exception of Church Street, the narrow road in today's cemetery, Nelson and Langtry Streets, none of the above mentioned new streets exist today. All lots were laid out in quarter acre and half acre lots with occasional divisions of unusual shapes and sizes. There were bridges drawn for the end of Langtry Street and Jane Street which at that time extended to the river.

Most of the new streets were named after Edward Webster's family. Tremayne is named for his first wife and Langtry for his second wife.

Laura is for his daughter, Susan Laura; Herbert for his son, George Herbert; and Kate is for Mary Kate Jane, another daughter. His last child, Arthur, was not born in 1861, and the only one of his family not remembered in Creemore's street names.

What is particularly interesting are the buildings that are marked on this map, some identified. Previously mentioned are the two grist mills. At the north west corner of Mill and George is the Wilcox Tavern, a building that still stands. There are two other taverns, Kelly's on the south east corner of Mill and Edward, and Gowan's on Edward Street. These two businesses are not listed in the 1861 assessment. Maybe the work was planned for the near future. There is a store on Mill Street, east side, and Langtry's shop across the street. Langtry's also have a machine shop near the Caroline Street bridge. The church is on the hill at the cemetery and the school is a little further south. Altogether there are twenty other buildings, probably mainly houses.

Of special interest are the roads west. Today's County Road 9 at the north end of the village is labeled as a "prospective gravel road." The road that was available for travel to the west was over the Caroline Street bridge. People travelled Caroline Street to the base of the hill where it turned south towards the fifth line and Mulmur, but here there was also a turn to the right. The road followed the south side of the river all the way to today's bridge over the Mad River in Websterville. From there it made its way to Dunedin.

This road was used for a number of years but there appears to be no record of its demise. There is an interesting comment about Rev. Forster, the Church of England minister and his family, who lived west of Creemore. "Any Sunday morning in the dry season he and his older children might be seen mounting their horses at the hitching-post in front of Claverleigh and riding together along the banks of the Mad river three miles to the bridge at Wellington Street."[2] This, of course, should be Caroline Street as Wellington Street does not go near the river.

The 1861 map may be found inside the back cover.

NOTES
1. The title of this map is <u>Village of Creemore</u>... part of lots 9 & 8 in the 4th & 5th concessions of the Township of Nottawasaga. The property of E. Webster, Esq. Surveyed by W. Sanders, P.L.S., 1861.
2. <u>The Gothic Rectory,</u> p. 19.

1861 CENSUS

Name	Occupation	Place of Birth	Religion	Age	House
Samuel Willcox	Innkeeper	Canada W.	C of E	34	Frame
Sarah Willcox	"	"	"	31	
Joseph Willcox	"	"	"	10	
Margaret Willcox		"	"	6	
Susan Willcox		"	"	3	
Elizabeth Willcox		"	"	2	
Catherine Morrow		"	"	16	
Robert Lambert	Labourer	Ireland	"	22	
John Naggs	Labourer	Canada W.	"	34	
George Webster	Builder	"	"	52[1]	
Christiana Cowan		England	"	57	Frame
Grace Cudmore		"	"	19	
John Cudmore		Canada W	"	13	
Christiana Cudmore		"	"	12	
George Friend		"	"	2	
Mary Friend		"	"	23	
James Friend			R.C.	18	
George Friend			R.C.	16	
Robert Duff	Joiner	Scotland	C of S	70	
H. Galloway	Framer	Canada W.	C of S	27	Frame
J. Campaign	Framer	Ireland	C of E	35	Frame
M. Campaign	"	"	"	30	
Geo. Campaign		Canada W.	"	16	
Thos. Campaign		"	"	14	
Sarah Campaign		"	"	12	
James Campaign		"	"	10	
M. A. Campaign		"	"	8	
E. J. Campaign		"	"	6	
William Casey	Blacksmith	Ireland	"	33	
E. C. Casey		United States	"	40	
Robert M. Woodruff		Canada W.	"	19	
Anson Woodruff		"	"	17	
M.J. Woodruff		"	"	15	

Name	Occupation	Place of Birth	Religion	Age	House
Charles E. Woodruff		"	"	13	
Elmina Casey		"	"	8	
Betsy Lyman		"	"	17	
John Martin	Machinist	Scotland	U. P.	74	Frame
Agnes Martin		Scotland	U.P.	70	
James Martin		"	"	34	
Edward Webster	Manufacturer	Canada W.	C of E	44	Frame
Mary Webster		Ireland	"	33	
Francis Webster		Canada W.	"	13	
Elizabeth Webster		"	"	12	
Caroline Webster		"	"	11	
Wellington Webster		"	"	9	
Susan Webster		"	"	5	
George Webster		"	"	4	
Kate Webster		"	"	2	
Patrick Delany	Labourer	Ireland	R.C.	44	Frame
Margaret Delany		"	"	36	
Mary Delany		"	"	15	
Margaret Delany		"	"	7	
Elizabeth Delany		Canada W.	"	3	
James Griffin	Blacksmith	Ireland	W. M.	25	
M. A. Griffin		"	"	21	
F. J. Griffin		Canada W.	"	3	
J. M. Griffin		"	"	1	
M. J. Corbutt		"	"	15	
James Kenny		"	C of E	19	
Stephen Lyman	Book Agent	"	E. M.	45	Log
Elizabeth Lyman		"	"	29	
Elizabeth Lyman		"	"	15	
M.A. Lyman		"	"	3	
G. J. Bolster	Merchant	Ireland	C of E	29	Frame
S. Bolster		"	"	75	
Ann Bolster			R. C.	63	
A.M. Bolster			C of E	27	

Name	Occupation	Place of Birth	Religion	Age	House
Sarah Bolster		"	R. C.	30	
Joseph Maroony		Canada W.	R.C.	14	
Thos. Kitching	Shoemaker	England	C of E	39	Frame
M. J. Kitching		Ireland	"	25	
M. A. Kitching		Canada W.	"	4	
James Dott	Shoemaker	Scotland	F. C.	37	
James Langtry	Turner	Ireland	C of E	55	Frame
Mary Langtry		"	"	52	
William Langtry	Carpenter	"	"	30	
James Langtry	Cabinet Maker	Ireland	C of E	24	
John Langtry	Carpenter	Canada W.	"	22	
Sophia Mason		England	"	13	
Grace Cudmore		"	"	19	
Susan Webster		Canada W.	"	5	
C. Thornbury	Cabinet Maker	"	"	17	
H. Ridgeway	Cabinet Maker	"	"	18	
Joshua Sykes	Fuller & Carder	England	C of S	66	Log
Sarah Sykes		"	"	66	
E. J. Springer		Canada W.	C of E	14[2]	

NOTES
1. The age for George Webster is incorrect. He was born in 1825.
2. Canada W - Canada West
   C. of E. - Church of England
   R.C. - Roman Catholic
   C. of S. - Church of Scotland
   U.P. - United Presbyterians
   W.M. - Wesleyan Methodists
   F. C. - Free Church

1861 ASSESSMENT

Name	Occupation	Age	Property
Allan Flack	Yeoman	22	S. Edward St., 15
Henry Galloway	Carpenter	30	S. Elizabeth St., 42, 43
Elijah Wilcox	Carpenter	33	N. Caroline St., 10, 11, 12.
Edward Webster	Postmaster	43	S. Edward St., 11, 12.
			Con. 4, N 1/2 7.
			Con. 4, pt. 8.
			Con. 4, SW pt. 9.
			Con. 5, pt. E 1/2 8.
			Con. 5, SW pt. 9.
Fraser and Webster	Millers	38	Mill Reserve,
		43	Con. 4, pt. 8.
George Webster	Miller	30	N. Edward St., 20, 21, 22.
			S. Edward St., 13, 14.
George J. Bolster	Merchant	26	N. Edward St., 13, 18, 19.
			S. Edward St., 16, 20, 21,
			22, 23.
			S. Elizabeth St., N 1/2 11 & 12.
			N. Elizabeth St., 42.
			Con. 4, NW pt. 9.
James H. Grant	Merchant	37	N. George St., 1.
Samuel Wilcox	Inn Keeper	33	N. George St., 2, 3.
John Martin Sen.	Yeoman	74	N. George St., 4, 5.
			S. Edward St., 17.
William Casey	Blacksmith	31	N. Edward St., 10, 11.
			S. Elizabeth St., S 1/2 11 & 12.
			Con. 3, E 1/2 8.
Thomas Kitching	Shoemaker	35	N. Edward St., 7, 8.
			S. Edward St., 6.
Christiana Cowan	Widow		Mill St., 12.
Stephan Lyman	M. Preacher	42	N. Caroline St., 51.
James Langtry Sen.	Turner	55	N. Caroline St., 53, 54, 55.
			S. Francis St., 56.
William Langtry	Turner	30	S. Francis St., 55.
James Langtry Jr.	Turner	25	S. Francis St., 54.
John Langtry	Turner	23	S. Francis St., 53.
Jane Saltry	Widow		N. Elizabeth St., 44.

A SHATTERED DREAM

Life the way it was came to an abrupt end for Edward Webster on July 7, 1862. He was 45, and the father of eight children, Arthur, the youngest only two months old. For almost twenty years he had fostered a dream of success, and had seen Creemore grow from a forested valley to a thriving village of at least 200. He had been responsible for bringing mills to accommodate the needs of the pioneers and had the ability and drive to formulate a plan for a village site. As well, he had risked borrowed money to do so.

Edward Webster's ambitions were not for financial success alone. He expended much energy for the good of the community. It was he who donated land for the first church and cemetery and served on the church's board of directors. The first classes for school children were in his home and he was among the first who served on the school board, lending money to keep the school open when grants and taxes did not come in. He opened a store and arranged for the first post office. Commanding respect, he also held the position of Magistrate.

Life had dealt Edward Webster a nasty blow when his wife, Elizabeth Ann, died in 1853. He arranged care for his young family and in 1855 he married a young woman from the village, Mary Langtry, who bore him two sons and two daughters. Edward Webster had met adversity and survived.

On July 7, 1862, he was served with foreclosure papers[1] by William Sanders of Barrie and other creditors. He was left with some lots on George, Mill, Edward, Elizabeth and Caroline Streets and 100 acres in lot 9, concession 5. The 100 acres was lost in 1865. Fortunately, there was a bit of good news. In July, 1868, he and a partner were able to sell the lots he owned in the village for $700.

Some time in the next year he left Creemore forever and moved to Toronto. His name does not appear in the Toronto Directory for 1863 but it is there in the 1864-65 directory. The family was living at 111 Mutual Street and the oldest son, Frank, was working as a bible salesman. The family moved every year or two, something that indicates financial hardship, and Edward's occupation changed just as regularly.

Why did all this happen? How did all the hard work and ambitious dreams come to naught? In 1857 he had taken out a mortgage for 2000 Pounds.[2] It is possible he had let bills pile up as well. Perhaps he was a poor manager. Perhaps the people who bought lots did not pay up, or maybe too many people bought on credit at his places of business. The heady excitement of the first railway to Collingwood may have had something to do with it. It has been suggested that"[g]reat things were expected of this unexpected enterprise, and the impetus it gave Nottawasaga was marvelous. The settlers began to borrow money through the security of mortgages on their farms. They were certain that with the prosperity fore-shadowed they could easily discharge the engagement, redeem the mortgage and meantime have the use of the money to improve their homes, and get a few luxuries which they and their wives deserved, for they were all economical and worked hard. This was their logic. They overlooked the fact that a mortgage much resembles a mastiff, when he takes hold it is hard to make him let go!"[3]

NOTES

1. Abstracts of concessions 4 and 5, Nottawasaga, Land Registry Office, Barrie.

2. See above.

3. Nottawasaga: The Outburst of the Iroquois, p. 80.

1866 ASSESSMENT

Name	Occupation	Age	Property
Robert Steele	Blacksmith	25	S. Geo. St., 1, 2 & 37.
Reuben Smith	Merchant	25	N. Geo. St., 1.
			S. Main St., 36, 37.
			Stayner
Thomas Galloway	Shoemaker	26	N. Edw. St., 17.
John Foster	Preacher	45	S. Caroline St., 13.
Elijah Wilcox	Carpenter	35	N. Caroline St., 10, 11, 12.
Henry Galloway	Carpenter	41	S. Elizabeth St., 42, 43.
William Gowan	Inn Keeper	25	W. Mill St., 31.
Samuel Wilcox	Yeoman	38	N. Geo. St., 2, 3.
Geo. C. McManus	M. D.	30	N. Edw. St., 3, 6.
			N. Elizabeth St., 2.
William Casey	Blacksmith	37	S. Elizabeth St., S 1/2 11 & 12.
			N. Edw. St., 10, 11.
			Con. 3 E 1/2 8.
Thomas Kitching	Shoemaker	43	S. Edw. St., 4.
John Campaign	Labourer	40	N. Elizabeth St., 42, 43.
William A. Graham	——	28	N. Elizabeth St., 44.
Stephan Lyman	Preacher	50	N. Caroline St., 51.
James Sidey	Labourer	31	N. Caroline St., 58, 59, 60.
			N. Laura St., 58, 59, 60.
Mrs. Cowan	Widow		N. Elizabeth St., 12.
James Langtry Sr.	Carpenter	58	Langtry's Block
William Langtry	Carpenter	31	Langtry's Block
James Langtry Jr.	Carpenter	29	Langtry's Block
John Langtry	Carpenter	26	Langtry's Block
John G. Martin	Inn Keeper	34	S. Edw. St., 13, 14, 15.
Wm Kelly,	Owner		N. Edw. St., 20, 21, 22.
			Collingwood
John G. Martin			S. Edw. St., 16, 17.
			N. Geo. St., 4, 5.
Oliver Cluson	Mason	40	N. Edw. St., 7, 8.
Robert Patterson	Saddler	27	N. Elizabeth St., 13.
John Coupland	Agent		N. Edw. St., 14, 15,

Name	Occupation	Age	Property
George J. Bolster	Merchant	33	S. Edw. St., 18-23 inclusive. N. Edw. St., 1, 2, 13, 18, 19. S. Elizabeth St., 1, 13, N 1/2 11&12 4th con., E 1/2 9. 4th con., N 1/2 of NW 1/4 9. 5th con., S 1/2 of NE 1/4 7.
Edward Webster of Toronto			N. Webster St., 1 to 13 inclusive. W. Herbert St., 14, 15 and that parcel of Land between Webster St., E. and Mountain St. with G. Mill and other Buildings, 4th con., pt. 8.

1871 CENSUS

Name	Age	Place of Birth	Religion	Origin	Occupation
McDonald, Duncan	34	N.S.	C. Scotland	Scotch	Minister
" Elloner	28	Q.	"	Irish	
" John	4/12	O.	"	Scotch	
Gillespie, Alexander	27	O.	R. Baptist	Scotch	Post Master
" Ann	71	Scotland	"		
" Mary	32				
" Florah	29	O.	"	"	
Royal, William	30	Scotland	W. Meth.	Irish	Labourer
" Dortas	30	England	"	English	
" William	12	O.		Irish	
" Albert	10	"	"	"	
" George	8	"	"	"	
Amandamum	6	"	"	"	
" Doetas	4	"	"	"	
" John	2	"	"	"	
McManus, George	31	O.	C. England	Irish	Doctor
" Jane	28	"	"	Scotch	
" Samuel	2/12	"	"	Irish	
McKinnon, Ann	21	"	Presb.	Scotch	Servant
Shaossell, Thomas	16	"	Catholic	French	"
Cudmore, John	23	"	Ep Meth.	English	Labourer
" Susan	20	"	"	"	
" William	1	"	"	"	
Murday, Robert	33	"	W. Meth.	Irish	Farmer
" Rachel	33	"	"	"	
" Tracey Ann	10	"	"	"	
Webb, John	30	"	C. C. Bapt.	German	Labourer
" Alice	29	"	"	"	
" Joseph	7	"	"	"	
" Anjaline	6	"	"	"	
" Arabella	2	"	"	"	
" Jane	55	Ireland	"	"	
Forster, William	43	England	C. England	English	Minister
" Clarissa	44	"	"	"	
" Claria	17	O	"	"	
" Agusta	14	"	"	"	

Name	Age	Place of Birth	Religion	Origin	Occupation
Forster, Lucy	13	O.	C. England	English	
" Charles	11	"	"	"	
" Louisa	8	"	"	"	
" Ann	6	"	"	"	
" George	4	"	"	"	
" Jennie	1	"	"	"	
Read, Sarah	21	"	"	"	
Graham, William	32	O	Ep. Meth.	Irish	Mason
" Christina	22	"	"	"	
" Mary	7	"	"	"	
" Maria	5	"	"	"	
" George	2	"	"	"	
Crain, John	75	Ireland	None	"	
Rayman, John	66	O	Ep. Meth.	Irish	Farmer
" Maria	59	Ireland	"	"	
" Maryjane	33	O	"	"	
" Curtis	30	United States		"	Labourer
" Freboen	25	O	"	"	
" Cecilla	2	"	"	"	
" Almina	19	"	"	"	
" Elizas	18	"	"	"	Labourer
Wilcox, Elija	40	O	W. Meth.	German	Carpenter
" Fanney	40	"	"	"	
" William	16	"	"	"	
" Edward	14	"	"	"	
" Mathew	11	"	"	"	
" Sarah	9	"	"	"	
" Margaret	7	"	"	"	
" Elizabeth	5	"	"	"	
" Susanna	2	"	"	"	
" Mary	1/12	"	"	"	
Taylor, Charles	47	England	Meth. E.	English	Clergiman
" Martha	47	O	"	"	
" Mary	18	"	"	"	
" Charles	16	"	"	"	
" Matilda	13	"	"	"	
" Abigail	11	"	"	"	
" Robert	6	"	"	"	
" Jane	3	"	"	"	

Name	Age	Place of Birth	Religion	Origin	Occupation
Gunn, Angus	55	O	Meth. E.	Scotch	Lumberman
" Mary	51	Scotland	Presb.	"	
" Ann	19	O	"	"	
" James	26	"	"	"	Merchant
" Christena	17	"	"	"	
" Mary	13	"	"	"	
" Hannah	11	"	"	"	
" Florah	6	"	"	"	
Kelley, William	44	Q	C. Scotland	Irish	Hotel Keeper
" Maryann	44	England	"	English	
Dyer, Annjain	9	O	"	"	
Nicely, David	30	O	C Scotland	German	Farmer
" Rebeca	27	"	"	"	
" Margaret	6	"	"	"	
" John	3	"	"	"	
" Mary	1	"	"	"	
Murday, Joseph	38	O	W. Meth.	Irish	Farmer
" Margaret	37	"	"	"	
" Rachel	6	"	"	"	
" James	4	"	"	"	
" Joseph	2/12	"	"	"	
Carleton, Maryann	40	Ireland	C. England	Irish	
" Franses	7	O	"	"	
" Mary	5	"	"	"	
" Samuel	4	"	"	"	
" Thomas	3	"	"	"	
Gowen, Ann	12	"	"	"	
" Samuel	3	"	"	"	
McRonald, Andrew	34	Ireland	W. Meth.	Irish	Weaver
" Martha	32	"	"	"	
" Maryann	14	"	"	"	
" James	12	"	"	"	
" Jane	10	"	"	"	
" Certillia	7	"	"	"	
" Matildia	6	"	"	"	
" Andrew	3	"	"	"	
" William	1	O	"	"	
" Elizabeth	2	"	"	"	
Patterson, Robert	33	Ireland	C. England	Irish	Saddler
" Ann	28	O	"	"	

Name	Age	Place of Birth	Religion	Origin	Occupation
Patterson, John	4	O	C. England	Irish	
Gowen, Christena	66	England	C. England	English	
Irwin, Thomas	29	O	C. England	Irish	Shoemaker
" Elizabeth	23	Ireland	"	"	
" Mary	1	O	"	"	
Montgomery, Jane	50	Ireland	"	"	
" Catharine	27	"	Presb.	"	
Kitchen, Thomas	58	England	C. England	English	Shoemaker
" Margaret	30	Ireland	"	"	
" Maryann	14	O	"	"	
" Maria	6	"	"	"	
" Thomas	4	"	"	"	
" Frances	10/12	"	"	"	
Baley, William	50	Ireland	C. England	English	Saddler
" Maryann	39	England	"	"	
" Eliza	19	O	"	"	
" Maryann	17	"	"	"	
" George	15	"	"	"	
" Louise	12	"	"	"	
" Jessie	10	"	"	"	
" William	5	"	"	"	
" Charles	3	"	"	"	
Lee, Sarah	21	O	C. England	Irish	Milliner
" Maria	22	"	"	"	
Clusin, Oliver	38	Norway	C. England	Norwegian	Mason
" Farina	38	"	"	"	
" Mary	16	O	"	"	
" Emme	12	"	"	"	
Wilcox, Samuel	42	O	"	German	Lumberman
" Sarah	39	Ireland	"	Irish	
" Joseph	19	O	"	German	
" Margaret	17	"	"	"	
" Susanna	13	"	"	"	
" Elizabeth	11	"	"	"	
" Jane	9	"	"	"	
" Sarah	6	"	"	"	
" Catharine	5	"	"	"	
" Maria	3	"	"	"	

Name	Age	Place of Birth	Religion	Origin	Occupation
McKay, John	25	O	C. Scotland	Irish	Merchant
" Elizabeth	28	"	"	Scotch	
" Alexander	1	"	"	Irish	
McArthur, Mary	64	Scotland	"	Scotch	
Smith, Ruben	28	O	C. C. Bapt.	English	Store Keeper
" Ann	28	"	"	Scotch	
" George	7	"	"	English	
" Danial	5	"	"	"	
" Christena	3	"	"	"	
" Maryann	1	"	"	"	
Sutherland, Alex	30	O	C. Scotland	Scotch	Hotel Keeper
" Martha	27	"	"	"	
" James	7	"	"	"	
" Catharine	2	"	"	"	
Steel, Robert	30	C. Scotland		Irish	Blacksmith
" Elizabeth	27	"	"	"	
" Catharine	5	"	"	"	
" Margaret	2	"	"	"	
" Alford	4/12	"	"	"	
Glenning, Edward	30	England	C. England	English	Miller
" Sarah	27	"	"	"	
" Emmey	9	O	"	"	
" George	9/12	"	"	"	
Fox, Christian	64	O	Ep. Meth.	Irish	Cooper
" Mary	57	Ireland	"	"	
" Peter	28	O	"	"	Labourer
" Edward	26	"	"	"	
" John	23	"	"	"	
" Christopher	19	"	"	"	
Brown, Martha	24	"	"	"	
" Edward	17	"	"	"	
Taylor, Matilda	4	"	"	"	
Haney, Patrick	25	Ireland	Catholic	Irish	Store clerk
Carew, Margaret	27	"	"	"	
Webb, Alonzo	27	O	Baptist	German	Labourer
" Elizabeth	24	"	"	English	
" Albert	5	"	"	German	
" Alonzo	3	"	"	"	
" William	1	O	Baptist	German	

RETURN OF INDUSTRIES
CREEMORE

#1
Flour mill, Phillip Low, proprietor; fixed capital-$1000; working months
in the year-12; average number of employees, male, over 16-2; males
under 16-1; aggregate amount of yearly wage-$360; power-water with
nominal force of 30; raw material-wheat, 10,000 bushels; aggregate
value- $10,200; products-flour, bran and shorts; aggregate value-
$17,000; remarks-only ????gristing

#2
Blacksmith forge, Robert Steel, proprietor; fixed capital invested-$300;
floating capital employed- $700; number of working months in the year-
12; average number of employees, male, over 16-2; aggregate yearly
wage-$300; raw material-iron, coal and steel; aggregate value-$700;
products- country work for farmers; aggregate value-$1700; remarks-
including repairs.

#3
Cloth factory, Ruben Smith, proprietor; fixed capital invested-$5500;
number of working months in the year-6; average number of employees,
male over 16-2; males under 16-2; power-water, nominal force of 15;
raw material-wool 5500 lb, carded wool, 4500 lb.; aggregate value-
$3750; products-cloth and carding, 4500 yards; aggregate value- $4500.

NOTES
N.S - Nova Scotia
Q. - Quebec
O. - Ontario
C. Scotland - Church of Scotland
R. Baptist - Regular Baptist
W. Meth. - Wesleyan Methodist
C. England - Church of England
Presb. - Presbyterian
Ep. Meth. - Episcopal Methodist
C.C. Baptist - Christian Conference Baptist
Meth. E. - Methodist Episcopal

1871 ASSESSMENT

As you can't help noticing, Philip Low seems to have taken over the most of the village. He was a lawyer living in Picton, Ontario. Unfortunately requests for information about Mr. Low have been unsuccessful. Why he ended up holding all this land in Creemore is a mystery yet. It had something to do with Edward Webster's foreclosure, but what?

At the end of this assessment you will find the number of people and the number of farm animals that were within the village boundaries. In the assessment they are listed separately for each residence. Here you will find the totals to give you the whole picture.

Philip Low, Occupation-N.R., from Picton, Ontario.
4th Con., pt. 7, S.E. pt 8
Block 2, pt. 7&8
Block 5, S.E. pt. 8 in 5th con.
Block 7, pt. 9 in 5th con.
Block G, pt. 8 in 5th con.
Part lot 34, S. Edward St.
Pt. lots 35 & 36, S.
Edward St.
Part lot 44, S. George St.
N. Caroline St., 1,2,3,4,5,
6,7,8,9.
N. Caroline St., 13 to 49
inclusive
S. Caroline St., 1 to 10
inclusive.
S. Caroline St., 14 to 25
inclusive.
S. Caroline St., 42 to 50
inclusive.
N. Edward St., 23 to 32,
62 to 65 inclusive.
S. Edward St., 1,2 & 24
to 33 inclusive.
N. Elizabeth St., 4 to 10,
16 to 26, 45 to 48 .
S. Elizabeth St., 2,4,5,7,8,

Name	Occupation	Age	Concession or Street & Lot
Philip Low, Occupation-N.R., cont'd			9,15,17,19 to 26, And 44 to 51 inclusive. N. Francis St., 2 to 10 & 13 to 24 inclusive. S. Francis St., 1 to 25 & 41 to 52 inclusive. N. George St., 9 to 15 & 32 to 36 inclusive. S. George St., 8 to 16 inclusive. W. Mary St., 19 to 22 inclusive. S. Nelson St., 1 to 11 inclusive. S. Wellington St., 1 to 25 inclusive. N. Wellington St., 2 to 12 inclusive.
Edward C. Glenning	Miller	34	Mill Reserve
Philip Low	N.R.		
Geo. Carson McManus	M.D.	30	N. Edward St. 4,5,6,7,8 S. Edward St. 8,9
Thomas Irwin	Shoemaker	26	S. Elizabeth St. Pt. 11, 12
Robert Steele	B'smith	26	W. Mill St. 37, 38 S. George St. 1,2
Thomas Galloway	Shoemaker	27	N. Edward St. 17
Samuel Wilcox	Agent	40	N. George St. 2,3
Edward & John McKay	Merchants	25	W. Mill St. 30
George Webster			
Alex'r Sutherland	Inn Keeper	30	W. Mill St. 31
Wm Gowan	N. R.		
Wm Kelly	Inn Keeper	45	S. Edward St. 13, 14, 15 N. Edward St. 19, 20, 21, 33, 34 4th Con. N.E. pt. 9 4th Con. pt. 8
James Hudson	Labourer	35	S. George St. 17, 18

Name	Occupation	Age	Concession or Street & Lot
Wm Casey	B'smith	40	N. Edward St. 10,11
Wm Casey (cont'd)			S. Elizabeth St.
			S 1/2 11,12
Charles Woodruff	Wagon maker	22	3rd Con. E 1/2 8
Alex'r Gillespie	Merchant	26	N. Edward St. 12
Wm Boyle	Labourer	30	S. Edward St. 11
Patrick Henry	Merchant	24	N. George St. 1
Wm Casey			
Christian Fox	Cooper	61	S. George St. 7
James Brown	Cooper	34	N. George St. 6,7
Henry Howie	Tinsmith	36	N. George St. 8
John Webb	Labourer	35	S. George St. Pt. 42
Alonzo Webb	Labourer	33	S. George St. Pt. 33
Mary Ann Carlton	Widow	——	S. Edward St. 16, 17
			N. George St. 4,5
George Townsend	Yeoman	35	S. George St. E. pt. 43
Henry Galloway	Carpenter	43	N. Edward St. 16
			Elizabeth St. 42, 43
Oliver Cluson	Mason	39	N. Wellington St.
			S. George St. Pt. 40
Thomas Kitching	Shoemaker	50	S. Edward St. 6
Arch'd McNabb	Carpenter	28	N. Caroline St. 50, 51
John McKay	Yeoman	40	S. Caroline St. Block C & F
William Langtry	Carpenter	39	S. Caroline St. Block D & E
Rueben Smith	Merchant	28	N. Edward St. 3
			S. George St. 3,4,5,6
			Pt. Langtry Block A & B
			E. Mill St. 13
Thomas Dunsheath	Clerk	22	N. George St. Pt. 41
			S. Edward St. 10, 12
James Brown	Yeoman	39	N. Caroline St. Pt.
			Langtry Bl.
			2nd Con. W 1/2 31
			2nd Con. 32
Robert Patterson	Saddler	32	N. Elizabeth St. 13,14,15

Name	Occupation	Age	Concession or Street Lot
Mrs. Cowan	Widow		W. Mill St. 12
Thomas Miller			N. Elizabeth St. 2,3
George Miller			
W.R. Forster	A.M.		
And'w T. McReynolds	Weaver	54	S. Edward St. Pt. 31
Wm Bailey	Saddler	49	S. Edward St. Pt. 32
Joseph Coupland	Yeoman	22	N. Edward St. 16,17
Thomas Dack	M.D.	28	N. Elizabeth St. 42,43
			N. Elizabeth St. 1
			S. Elizabeth St. 1
			N. Edward St. 1
Sarah Lee	Spinster	——	S. Caroline St. 13
Elijah Wilcox	Carpenter	——	S. Caroline St. 10,11,12

There were 171 individuals listed but these are only the ones who lived on their own property. The renters are not included. Animals listed included 28 head of cattle, 6 sheep, 17 hogs and 9 horses. Dr. McManus had two horses for his round of house calls and William Kelly had four, probably for hire, as he had a hotel.

Photos in clockwise direction
beginning at the right:

Judge James R. Gowan
*Photo courtesy of the Simcoe
County Archives*

Edward Webster
*Photo from the collection of Helen
Emmett Blackburn*

William Gowan
*Photo from the collection of Helen
Emmett Blackburn*

In clockwise direction beginning above:

Prince of Wales honoured guest on the Ontario, Huron and Simcoe Railway, 1860.
Photo from the collection of John Hollingworth, photographer, Toronto.

George Webster
Photo from the collection of Helen Emmett Webster

Mrs. Bridget Dowling and her daughter, Mary Giffen Mrs. Dowling named the Mad River. Her daughter was a baby in arms in the day Mrs. Dowling nearly lost her life crossing the Mad River at Glen Huron.
Photo courtesy of Agnes Douglas

Henrietta and John
McDonald

married 1831

1807 ~ 1900   1787 ~ 1860

<u>John McDonald</u> *(above)* This sketch of Henrietta and John McDonald is copied from portraits hanging in John McDonald House, Gananoque.

<u>John McDonald House</u> *(below),* built 1830, was the elegant home of Henrietta and John McDonald in Gananoque. Recent renovations have recaptured its original style. It is used as Gananoque's Town Hall.

Drawings courtesy of the Town of Ganonoque

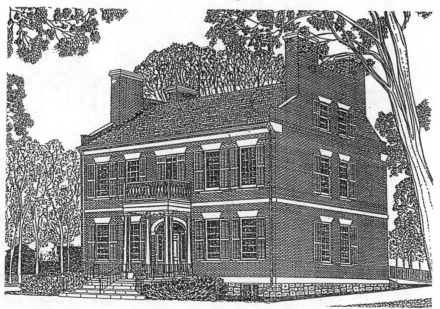

The Cottage School *(above)* built by John Kendrick and Mick Steed in 1852. Photographed in 1905.
Photo from the collection of Helen Emmett Blackburn
The Anglican Church, *(below)* built on the hill at the cemetery.
Photocopied from <u>100 Years of History: St. Luke's, Creemore</u>

The Josephine one of the original engines on the Ontario, Huron and Simcoe Railway that pulled trains from Toronto to Collingwood.

Photo courtesy of the Simcoe County Archives.

The Anglican Church

Wilcox Inn

The Orange Hall

Residence of W. Casey

Clockwise beginning on the right:

Home of Edward Webster

The Mill

Kelly's Hotel

Photos courtesy of Donald Webster

Map legend:

1. Grist and Flour Mill
2. Saw Mill, Carding & Fulling Mill, Bedstead and Chair Factory
3. House- Edward Webster
4. General Store, dry goods, hardware & groceries, Post Office 5. Stable 6. Potash Works 7. House 8. Blacksmith Shop 9. Tannery 10. John Kendrick, millwright's house and shop 11. Creemore Inn and driving house 12. House- George Webster 13. W. Casie- blacksmith shop and house 14. Dam 15. Dam 16. Waste gate

Map of the Southern Section of Nottawasaga Township
Notice the extension of Caroline Street that runs south of the river to Websterville, and the extension of Edward Street that runs south east. This map is a ready reference for the lots and concessions referred to in the text.

Map copied from the Belden Atlas

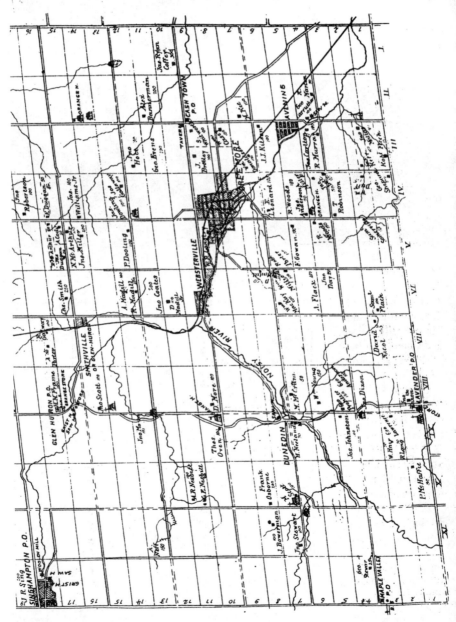

CREEMORE'S FIRST DOCTOR

There was nothing adventurous or romantic about the hardships of pioneer life. Doctors usually lived miles and miles away. People knew how to use herbs, there were midwives, although officially untrained and most people had a medicine cabinet for emergencies. But when a crisis occurred there were only prayers and a glass of whiskey. The arrival of a doctor in Creemore must have been a welcome event. But when you get to the end of this account you may wonder to yourself about the stress placed upon the doctor himself.

The account of Creemore's earliest doctors first appeared in the Creemore Star of at least fifty years ago and the writer seemed to be making guesses about some of these men. It was stated that Dr. McManus was the first doctor here in the 1850s. The time frame does not appear to be correct. The 1871 census lists him as being 31 and it would be unlikely that he would have completed training even by 1859.[1] He was not listed in the 1861 census.[2] The 1850s map of Creemore indicates all the buildings and there is no Doctor's house.[3] However, he is listed in Orange Lodge record books as joining October 12th, 1865.[4]

Dr. George McManus came from a highly regarded family in Mono Township. His father, also George McManus, came to Canada somewhere around 1820. He became Reeve of Mono, Warden of Simcoe County (Mono was once part of Simcoe County), Conservative member of the Provincial Legislature and was divisional Court Clerk for his area.[5]

Dr. McManus was married to Jane, whose maiden name we do not know. The old article from the Creemore Star says he lived on Edward Street across from the Orange Hall, a building that is no longer the Orange Hall but still looks like one. The 1871 census tells us they had a son, Samuel, age two months. A short time before Samuel was born, their first-born son, Stuart Henderson McManus died. His gravestone in the Creemore Cemetery is engraved with 1871 and "only son of G.C. and J.S. McManus."[6]

The doctor's story has a sad ending. According to the Orangeville Sun of June 4, 1874, "Dr. G. C. McManus, son of Mr. G. McManus, died suddenly, at his residence in Newmarket, on Wednesday, the 27th of May. The deceased had returned from Toronto on Tuesday, and feeling unwell, went into his surgery, and took some morphine to induce sleep. He unfortunately took an overdose, and, notwithstanding that everything was done that medical skill could suggest, he died from the effects of the poison on the following morning. Dr. McManus was very highly respected by all who knew him, and his death will be sincerely regretted by a large circle of friends and acquaintances."[7]

NOTES

1. 1871 census
2. 1861 census
3. Map, <u>Creemore, the Property of Edward Webster</u>, by William Gibbard, 1853.
4. Royal Arch Purple Lodge No. 704, Creemore, members 1856-1943, minutes 1860-1950.
5. <u>The Northern Advance,</u> Barrie, 27 Oct. 1887, p. 1.
6. Index, Creemore Union Cemetery.
7. <u>Orangeville Sun</u>, June 4, 1874.

THE ORANGE LODGE

Forty or fifty years ago the 12th of July was a major holiday, not just for members of the Orange Lodge, but for almost everyone. It was the one event that prompted hard-working farmers to leave their haying. Vehicles could be seen from the earliest morning hours making their way to the locale of that year's parade. That village would be alive with fluttering flags and banners and church or other groups rushing about to prepare meals for the crowds.

In the Creemore area the Orange Lodge was quick to organize and was followed by many others. "In Leeds and Lansdowne townships [birthplace of Edward and George Webster] the Orange Order was by far the largest lodge or club and individual lodges were thicker on the ground than were the houses of worship of any single denomination."[1] This was true in Nottawasaga as two lodges were formed in 1849 before the first church was built in 1855, that of Creemore Anglican. How much longer this state of affairs lasted has not been determined but it is certain the Orange Lodge played an important role in the lives of our local pioneers.

As Orange Lodges are not as common as they once were it might be worthwhile to examine their appeal. First of all, think of the first settlers living a lonely existence often miles from the nearest neighbour. All day long the men worked at demanding physical labour: chopping trees, building shelters, grubbing roots from the soil in order to plant some grain, and tending a few farm animals. Most of the early settlers in Nottawasaga came from more populous areas where social interaction was the norm. And they missed it here. A reason to meet with others once a month had great appeal. They would get together, go through the club rituals, reaffirm their beliefs, smoke their pipes, drink whiskey and talk. Added to this was the fact that the organization wasn't ethnic or denominational in religion (excepting Roman Catholics). As well, the Orange Lodges were important as sources of business and job contacts and was a mutual-aid organization before the days of insurance. Many a young widow received help from her late husband's lodge.[2]

There was another side to the Orange Order. While there was no formal statement, there was a relationship with John A. Macdonald and the Conservative party.[3] For example, it has been noted that the "Orange influence had so infected the political process in Simcoe County that the poll could not proceed without violence." [4] This was in the days before the secret ballot. Also, stories abound of the anti Catholic behaviour, particularly on the 12th of July, the day for parades and celebrations. "[N]ewspaper reports of local Orange celebrations almost always took pains to make it clear that no sectarian disturbance was involved,"[5] thus implying that it was entirely possible.

There were five basic levels within the order: Orange, Purple, Blue, Royal Arch Mark, and Royal Scarlet. Each required a fee and an initiation ceremony.[6] It was from this list of degrees that the Purple Hill Lodge took its name and ultimately the farming community on the Fourth Line south of Creemore was named Purple Hill.

Some local accounts of the Orange Lodge have listed Purple Hill as #198. This number is likely a typographical error. The number is 193. Some original certificates from the Lodge have 193 written on them.[7]

There is very little information about the Purple Hill Lodge. A call to the Orange Lodge headquarters in Toronto brought no new information. There is a list of early lodges in Simcoe County that shows two warrants from Nottawasaga July 9, 1849.[8] One is listed as Duntroon, Nottawasaga; the other as just Nottawasaga. Early accounts tell us that Isaac Woods was the leader and the first master.

In the Belden Atlas of 1881[9] a tiny building with "Orange H." under it is on the north west corner of lot 4, concession 4. This location was on the east side of the Fourth Line. No information seems available on how long this lodge and building remained in existence. The certificate issued to David McCutcheon of Purple Hill Lodge is dated 30th November, 1888, which would indicate that the lodge was still in existence at that date.

Parades were not features in the very early 12th of July celebrations. Rather, the members walked to the home of one of their group. One early account tells of Mr. Galloway hosting the group. "The fatted calf had been slain and the crudely constructed but well laden tables in the forest around the Galloway home were soon the scene of great feasting."[10]

As Creemore grew, plans were made to open a lodge in the village of Creemore itself . A warrant was issued to Jno. Carleton, July 14, 1856, and the lodge given the number, 704.[11] The group built a hall on Edward

Street. When erected there was no basement although it was added later. The hall still stands on Edward Street, its return eaves revealing its 1850s origin.

Unfortunately the early record books from Creemore's lodge, # 704, are missing. If they should be found many interesting details and observations could be made.

NOTES

1. The Irish in Ontario: A Study in Rural History, page 278.
2. See above, page 277.
3. The Spread of the Loyal Orange Lodge Through Ontario, 1830-1900, page 15, available at the Ontario Archives.
4. Upper Canada Orangeism in the 19th Century, page 62, available at the Ontario Archives.
5. The Irish in Ontario, p. 278.
6. Upper Canada Orangeism in the 19th Century, p. 10.
7. The transfer certificate of David McCutcheon and Robert Rhodes have the number 193 and Purple Hill Lodge written on them. These are in the Simcoe County Archives, Midhurst, ON.
8. From the pamphlet, "The Story of Orangeism," available in the Ontario Archives.
9. The Illustrated Atlas of the County of Simcoe 1881, p. 33.
10. Creemore Tweedsmuir History, p. 90, in Creemore Public Library.
11." The Story of Orangeism."

SCHOOL DAYS

The following information about schooling for the children of Creemore and the surrounding district is taken from <u>Has the Bell Rung Yet?</u> , written by your author, under the name, Helen Hargrave, in 1979. The account of the first log school has not been changed but the rest has been rewritten. A great deal of information for that 1979 book came from the School Board Minute Book, now stored at the Clearview Municipal Office, Stayner.

THE FIRST LOG SCHOOL
This article was written by, F.E. Webster, and appeared in the January 9th 1936 issue of the Creemore Star.

I remember hearing my father tell me of the first efforts of the pioneers to provide a school. These early settlers felt it was their plain duty to make some provision to have their boys and girls taught at least primary education, that is, the three "R's". The old spirit of co-operation still prevailed among these brave men. They got together and settled the problem by all turning out and with the help of a team of oxen and sharp axes, they built a log school in one day. Within a short time a fireplace was built to keep the children warm in cold weather, and other equipment provided. The school was then ready to function. This all happened before school sections were organized in the Township of Nottawasaga in the early 50's. This enterprise was accomplished, not by seeking doles or help from government or other outsiders, but was the accomplishment of a patriotic community spirit. What a pity we have not retained this spirit!

On Fair day I met an old revered friend, Mr. John Mackay. After the usual salutations our conversation naturally drifted back to pioneer days. He being the only man living who was a pupil who attended the pioneer school, I was anxious to learn something about it. This school was situated a few rods from the northwest corner of the north half of lot 7, Concession 4 on the north side of what was known then as Wench's Hill. At this date there was no cut through that gully hill, and the people on the Fourth Line travelled in an easterly direction on Sideroad 6 missing the worst of the hill, from thence across the Powell farm, east of the Cemetery, entering Mill Street below where the Mill stood. Mr. Mackay travelled a different road when going to school. His home being on Lot 6, Concession 6, he travelled east until he came to the Steed farm, where he crossed over reaching the Kendrick farm, and thence to the Fourth Line.

Let us get back to the school. The desks in this school were fastened on the outer walls and the pupils sat on long benches facing the walls. There was a big fireplace that would take a block of wood five feet long. This big fireplace kept them warm in cold weather. Two different teachers, Mr. Hill and Mr. Monteith, taught while Mr. John Mackay attended. Some of the pupils who attended that school were Allan Flack, Solomon Millsap, Jacob Millsap, Edward John Millsap, James Ross, R. Dennis, Robert Rhodes, Josiah Rhodes, one of the Rhodes girls, John Kendrick, Elizabeth Kendrick (Mrs. Berry), Tom Woods, Edward Mackay and John Mackay.

Mr. Mackay remembers spending happy days at this little log school and saw some stirring events. He recalled seeing one of the bigger boys and the teacher settling their differences by pounding each other's heads. He related that it was nearly all bush from his home to his school and he had a horror of meeting Indians. One morning he met a man whom he thought at first was an Indian. He did not know at first whether to run for home or to face him. He worked up enough courage, however, to face him, but it turned out to be one of the Leonard boys who offered to treat him with something a little stronger than soda water. The writer was particularly grateful to get this information from the only man living who could give it. Only for him, none of us would have any record of the first school, where it was situated and its architecture. And after all, we at this age can endure the fact, that they turned out worthy Canadian citizens that were a credit to themselves and the community in which they lived.

Some teachers Mr. Mackay remembers in the first log school, Mr. Monteith and Mr. Hill. In the Cottage School, known as the Wench House, first Mr. Hill; second, Mr. Munson; then William Miller, Angus Bell and Malcolm Currie.

THE COTTAGE SCHOOL

This account of the second school was put together with the information gleaned from an article written by Mr. H.M. Corbett in 1946 and from the memories of Alice Emmett and Gordon Webster.

In 1854, the school was formally organized. It was School Section No. 6, Nottawasaga, and the first school board members were James Wilcox Sr., John Matchett, John Day and Edward Webster. The section included the area south of Creemore to the Town Line and west to the Sixth Line.

The organizational meeting was held March 4th, 1854. It was decided at the first meeting that the school should open May 1st and remain open for six months of the year. The records do not mention a school building until 1855, when a school was built on a site on the west side of the road just south of the Cemetery, or more precisely, on the north-east corner of Lot 7, Concession 5. The site for this school was presented to the section by the Hon. John McDonald. The school was built by J. Kendrick assisted by M. Stead and his contract price was 80 pounds.

A rather faded picture of the school shows a square, clapboard building with a cottage roof which is why it is referred to as the Cottage School. A narrow door is in the middle of one side and a small square window in another wall. From the roof protrudes a chimney which would indicate that it was heated with a stove rather than a fireplace. There was no foundation. The school was held up by posts at the corners. Frank Webster remembered how they used to crawl under the school.

We can't see the inside of the school but a description of the school at Duntroon written by Donald Blair will provide us with an aid to our imagination.[1] "...The master's desk was at the south end near the door. There were seats all around, a place along the front of the school for those who were learning to write, and also rows of seats in the middle. The seats were made of split basswood hewed smooth or planed, about three inches thick, and twelve inches wide with legs, and some of them were ten or twelve feet long. There was a first book and the new Testament was used as the Second Book. The higher classes used the Bible and English Reader and Speller. One would have to be able to read well before he was taught to write or cipher. The pens were made of goose quills as there were no steel pens at that time, but there were good penmen and also good readers."

Teachers were hard to get and one who stayed a year was an oddity. Often they were old soldiers. Most had only common school education and no teacher training. They had to establish their position by licking some of the older boys who challenged them. Wages were meagre, $100 to $300 if they could get it, and to earn it they had to look after the upkeep of the school in addition to keeping school.

At the first each pupil was required to pay one shilling per month. This rule prevailed until 1865, when, as the Creemore School Board minutes state, the Free School system was adopted. Provision was also made that each family that sent children to school should provide wood for heating purposes according to the number of children sent to school. This system existed until 1860 when tenders were asked to provide the wood. The contract was secured by W. Leonard at 75 cents a cord.

The balance of the expense was to be assessed on the property of the section. Taxes were not as easily collected then as they are today, for the minutes of the year 1856 state the Board was unable to collect 12 pounds and an appeal was made to the Township for aid as Mr. Ed Webster was out of pocket this amount, he having financed the school through the year.

The minutes of 1855 inform us that 77 pupils, ages 8 to 16, were enrolled that year. This seems like quite a large school for one teacher but one must realize that attendance was seldom more than 50 percent. There is nothing to indicate who the first teacher was, except for an entry in the cash book which reads, "Paid Mr. Archer 27 pounds."

The first teacher mentioned in any way in the minutes was Mr. Angus Bell and in the minutes of 1866 a form of agreement is shown wherein the Board agrees to hire Mr. Bell at a salary of 70 pounds a year but that he must first appear before the County Board of Education to prove that he is qualified for the position.

Many entries in the minute book remind us that great changes have taken place. In 1856 John Nevill was given the job of hauling something to the school with his oxen. The collecting of postage on delivery was still in vogue and we find that the Secretary paid one shilling on a letter received from Angus Bell. The transition from the sterling currency system to the decimal system that resulted in the school cash book getting badly out of balance; so much so, that in 1863 the matter was brought to the attention of Egerton Ryerson, then Provincial Superintendent of Education, and Mr. G. T. Bolster was appointed to audit the books for six years back.

In 1870 a school was built on the Fifth Line on lot 6, concession 6, the north-east corner. The teachers in this new Fifth Line School were George Stacey, Robert Little and R. M. Richmond. School continued in this building until it got too small. Then the School Board reopened the Cottage School again. Mrs. John Sidey recalled that she went to a school on George Street that was opened by Annie Bailey so the little tots would not have to climb up to the Fifth Line School. When the Cottage School was opened up a second time the first teacher was Miss Maggie Campbell of Duntroon; second, Miss MacDonald, who married Angus Gillespie, postmaster; third Miss Elizabeth Nesbitt; fourth, Miss Caswell.

School Section No. 6 operated two schools until 1881 when the section was divided into Mount Zion and Creemore. Those attending the Cottage School and still residing in the Creemore area in 1946 were Cassie, Bob and Alfred Steele, Isaac and John Woods, Albert Sidey, Mrs. W.D.Allen, Mrs. John Sidey, Robert Steed, Alma Weatherup, Mrs. Bob Royal, Mrs. John Boyd, John Carlton, George Hannah, John, William and Oswald Jardine, Francis Gowan and F. E. Webster.

Not long after the school was established in Creemore, money was set aside for the purchase of books to be given to pupils as prizes. It was a common practice for members of the community to attend the oral examinations held in the school, usually at the end of the school term. Prizes and promotions were awarded to the pupils excelling on that day. In 1867 they ran into considerable lack of interest on the parents' part so the School Board resorted to rather underhanded tactics to get the people into the school. The minutes stated, "Moved that prize books be supplied for this school for the ensuing year but that said prizes be not given to the children unless at least 10 heads of families attend the examinations."

NOTES

1. Nottawasaga: The Outburst of the Iroquois, p. 38

THE ANGLICAN CHURCH

The first Anglican Church is an attractive building. The graceful spire and the columns at the front must have been a treat for the settlers used to rude log cabins. The account of this church comes from <u>100 Years of History: St. Luke's, Creemore.</u>[1] It was written by Bert Smith, a church member and editor of the <u>Creemore Star.</u> He was able to use the birth register and the minutes as written by various vestry clerks. These books are now safely stored in the Anglican Archives, Toronto. As you read keep in mind that this was written in 1955.

Church of England missionaries working from an established mission in Mono Township and also from Bond Head where Rev. Mr. Osler had built a church, soon heard of the new settlement. [Creemore] According to the records, first Anglican services were held in private homes in 1846. Later, about 1850, services were held in the Orange Hall then situated two miles south of the present village.

Among the first missionaries who came to Creemore, preached the Gospel, baptised children and officiated at marriages, were Rev. George Bowen, Rev. John Fletcher, Rev. A. Hill, Rev. Mr. Osler.

Births were evidently numerous at that time and parents brought their babies to be baptised whenever a travelling preacher visited the newly started village. The first recorded baptisms were on January 18, 1846, when Rev. George Bowen received eleven infants into the Church. The family names of several of those who first sought the sacraments of the Church are familiar in the surrounding area one hundred years later, viz., Shields, Leach, Hewson, McCutcheon, Webster, Lounds, Morrison, Beatty, Brown, Bailey, Thomas, Wilson, Day, Perry, Honeyford, Steed, Boyes, Millie, Allen, Madill, Carlton, Siddall, Lott, Manning, Wilcox, Matchett, Coe, Kidd, Hamilton, Thornbury, Gowan, Irwin, Jones and Rhodes.

It was in the early spring of 1853 that a group of pioneer residents in Creemore area were convened to discuss ways and means for the erection of a place of worship. The population in the district was rapidly increasing as more and more settlers acquired land, or homesteads, as they preferred to call their holdings. Everywhere one looked it was virgin forest except for small clearings adjacent to the log cabins which were the pioneer homes. Mr. Edward Webster donated the site for a Church and a Cemetery.

A subscription list was opened by Mr. Webster at his mill which was evidently the hub of the community, and one of the very first contributions made toward the first proposed church was a bag of wheat (128 pounds) from William Millie, a 21-year-old homesteader who had located on the Fifth Line about 1 1/2 miles from the proposed church site. The wheat donation was accepted at the mill and the donor was credited with 14 shillings, 9 pence ($3.45). This was considered a generous donation at that time. It is probable that it came from the first wheat crop harvested by the young settler. Throughout his life he was a pillar in the church as has been his son and namesake 100 years later.

Mr. Millie, born in England, had been well nurtured in church activities. While a mere youth his father, who was one of the Governors of the Bank of England, was murdered while at work in the bank. He left a son and a daughter. The two children became wards of Mr. and Mrs. Williams who were an upper class English family. The Williams' daughter was the wife of Rev. Mr. Osler, who had been sent to Canada about 1830 by the Society for the Propagation of the Gospel. Mr. Osler founded the church at Bond Head and is said to have been one of the first ministers of the church to visit the Creemore settlement. In the late forties Mr. and Mrs. Williams, accompanied by the two Millie children, came from England to visit the Oslers at Bond Head. The Millie boy announced his ambition to acquire land and was directed by the land officials to come to South Nottawasaga where there were crown lands still available. He secured the patent for the north half of Lot 6, Con. 6, becoming a settler in 1851 at the age of 19. His foster parents, Mr. and Mrs. Williams, as well as the Rev. Mr. Osler, had an abiding interest in their ward. They were shocked when they learned there was at the time no church for him to worship in. Accordingly they got behind the movement. The Williams family promptly donated 10 pounds, or nearly $50.00.

Inspired by early contributions, in 1853 the promoters decided to go ahead with the building and in 1854 the contract was given to one John Kendrick for a consideration of 166 pounds (approximately $800.00). Mr. Kendrick engaged a local carpenter, Mr. Michael Steed, to assist him.

The Church, which was designated St. Luke's, Parish of Nottawasaga, was completed early in 1855. No record can be found regarding the first service but in the list of expenditures there is a record of the purchase of a stove on February 21st, 1855. It is presumed the new church was a reality in the spring of 1855.

It was no doubt through the influence of Rev. Mr. Osler of Bond Head that a promising and highly educated young missionary, The Rev. John Langtry, newly arrived from England, was sent as the first Incumbent of St. Luke's. [Correction: he was born in Ontario. His parents were from Ireland. See further notes at the end of this piece.][2] His parish was large, including Nottawasaga, Sunnidale and parts of Mulmur and Tosorontio Townships. Even before St. Luke's Church was completed Mr. Langtry faced the opportunity of a wider field for his talents. The railroad, under construction for two years, was completed to its terminus at Collingwood early in 1855. Expansion at the new port which promoters visualized as another Chicago, attracted residents by the hundreds. Among others, was Mr. Langtry, who in February, 1855, commenced holding church services in private homes. He founded All Saints' Church there and also founded a secondary school which later grew into a collegiate. Mr. Langtry soon established a home at Collingwood, but continued as the Incumbent of St. Luke's until 1862.

As the building of St. Luke's progressed the contributions towards its cost gradually came in. There was little outside assistance except for 12 pounds from the Church Society and the 10 pounds contributed by the Williams family. Edward Webster contributed 15 pounds but the majority of the contributions were for one pound and likewise several for 10 shillings.

From the first records we learn that the stipend which the first wardens of the church agreed to pay the Rev. John Langtry, their first appointed Incumbent, was 12 pounds. He had, of course, other sources of revenue. For instance the glebe income. Because St. Luke's was the first church built in Nottawasaga it was assigned a grant of land under the Clergy Reserves Act. It was specified in the act that the income only from this grant would go to the duly appointed Incumbent of the church in perpetuity. The glebe mentioned was sold and the proceeds (about $4000) was invested by the Synod of Toronto. However much to the chagrin of the officials of St. Luke's the Incumbent, Rev. Mr. Langtry, arranged that this annual income from the investment was divided with All Saints' Church, Collingwood, which was established by him the same year.

When the church was built and opened for worship in 1855 it was still far from completed. The interior had not been plastered and there were only benches for seats. In 1860 Mr. William Manning, who was the people's warden, made a special canvass for the purpose of raising funds to do a plastering job. Mr. Manning evidently supervised the job and rendered a detailed account,amounting to $73.30 for the completed job. The inventory by present day standards is quite interesting. For instance 4000 lath cost $8.00. Mr. Cluson, the plasterer, charged $44.00 for lathing and plastering. Other incidentals, including $1.25 to a char-woman who cleaned up the church, made up the amount.

In 1870 Rev. Forster became the first resident minister and built his well known home, Claverleigh, at the forks of the Mad and Noisy Rivers west of Creemore. The days of Rev. Forster and his family at Creemore make up a well loved story. But it is not for this book. It is for the next one.

NOTES

1. 100 Years of History: St. Luke's, Creemore 1855-1955

2. John Langtry was born at Palermo, Ontario, after his parents came to this country from Ireland. He was also educated in Ontario. This information is from the book. Two Hundred Years of Langtry History, 1761-1960. More information about John Langtry may be found in Diocese of Toronto Synod Journal, 1907, pp. 39-40, and A Brief Historical Survey of the Parish of St. Luke, Toronto, 1870-1955. These histories are available at the Anglican Archives, Toronto. A photograph of John Langtry hangs in one of the hallways at the Anglican Church in Collingwood.

THE PRESBYTERIAN CHURCH

Creemore has four churches at the present time but in the past there were several different denominations representing each church. As you read you will find out about the different Presbyterians who lived in Creemore and area.

There was no Presbyterian Church in the village of Creemore until 1876. Within the village limits the number of adherents was small. Including the two major Presbyterian denominations, the Church of Scotland and the Presbyterians, there were only seven members in the 1861 census, and 34 in the 1871 census. However, in 1871 the Church of Scotland minister, Duncan McDonald, resided in Creemore. This indicates the need for a Presbyterian minister somewhere near. That somewhere was Purple Hill. It was the gathering place for the Church of Scotland adherents and probably the Presbyterians from Creemore and around the countryside.

An especially interesting two-part account of the Presbyterian Churches at Purple Hill and in Creemore appears in two issues of the Creemore Star, December 18 and 25, 1913. It is far too long and has too many interesting stories of the churches to fit in this book. You are encouraged to read it on the microfilm at Creemore Library. It begins in the following manner. "The origin of Creemore Presbyterian church does not go back to Adam, but it does begin with an Isaac. In 1845 a sturdy Irish Canadian, Isaac Woods, his wife and child invaded the wilderness of South Nottawasaga and located on the old homestead of Purple Hill."

The Presbyterians made use of itinerant missionaries and met in homes until finally they were ready to have their own church and minister. On January 20, 1864, Alex McArthur sold to the Trustees of the Presbyterian Church of Canada a 1/4 acre lot for $100. This lot was on the northwest corner of his property, the west 1/2 of the north 1/2 of lot 4, concession 4.[1] Quite likely, the building of the church got underway that summer. There is not a trace of the building today, not a rock pile or a depression in the ground where the building might have been.

The following is an account of the church probably written for the 1946 Centennial Celebration. "According to Mrs. Robert Royal the first Presbyterian Church was a frame building on the north corner of lot 4 on the Fourth Line. Mrs. Royal was not old enough to go to school but old enough to go to Sunday School when the church was built. The approximate time of building would be about 1863. Mr. Isaac Woods, father of Mrs. Royal, was one of the leaders working for the church. Pioneer Carruthers who came to Banda in 1851 built the pulpit and carried it on his back up to the new church on the Fourth Line."

The family listed in the 1861 census as Presbyterian was United Presbyterian. It was in that same year that the United Presbyterians and the Free Church or Kirk united to become Canada Presbyterian Church. The Church of Scotland then united with this group in 1875.[2]

The Church of Scotland was more left wing in its style of worship and had a broader approach to religion. The Presbyterians, in contrast, were right wing and had a narrower approach. The people in this area must have set aside their theological differences before the parent churches did.[3]

The closest Presbyterian Church before 1864 was the East Nottawasaga Church north of Creemore, about five miles away. It was built in 1854 and its adherents were mainly Highland Scotch. Their services were often held in Gaelic.[4]

It was a long way to church in those days but the need for spiritual uplifting was strong. It was also a time for a little socializing, something they had little of as they worked on their isolated homesteads. Mrs. H. E. Fraser of Banda often told a story about her husband's ancestor who walked the many miles gladly to the East Nottawasaga Church. A phone call to Ross, her son, confirmed that this story was accurate. The woman concerned was Mrs. John Fraser, born Mary Campbell, who came with her husband in 1864 to the Fifth Line of Mulmur about a mile and a half south of the townline. On Friday she would walk to the East Nottawasaga Church a distance of about nine miles. Her route took her across a trail through the forest from the townline to the Fourth of Nottawasaga, through Creemore and up over the hills. Once there she would visit friends and attend a Friday evening service, stay over Saturday and go to church once more on Sunday. Her husband would come on Sunday with transportation and take her home. As the Frasers were Highland Scotch and the services in Gaelic this was probably the attraction because in her travels she would pass the new Presbyterian Church at Purple Hill.

After the congregation agreed to move into the village of Creemore and build a new church the old building on Purple Hill was used as an Orange Hall, then a barn and finally passed to dust and ashes by an accidental fire.[5]

NOTES

1. Abstracts for the Fourth Concession, Nottawasaga Township, Land Registry Office, Barrie, Ontario.

2. Genealogy in Ontario, p. 45.

3. Archivists, Presbyterian Archives, Toronto, Ontario, telephone interview, March 1999.

4. Nottawasaga: The Outburst of the Iroquois, p. 77.

5. Creemore Star, December 25, 1913.

THE METHODIST CHURCH

An excellent source of information about the Methodist churches is a thesis written by Rev. Glen Eagle. It was carefully researched, the sources cited and makes interesting reading. It may be found in Creemore Library. Rev. Eagle was the United Church minister in Creemore in the 1940s. At the time, he was studying for his Bachelor of Divinity degree and this thesis, Methodist Beginnings in Nottawasaga Township, was one of the requirements.[1]

Like the Baptists and the Presbyterians there were different branches of Methodists in Creemore. One was Wesleyan Methodist and the other Methodist Episcopal. There were also the Primitive Methodists who later joined up with the Methodist Episcopals. The Wesleyans and the Episcopals amalgamated in 1883 to make a larger, stronger church. The United Church of modern times has in its roots Methodist beginnings among others.

In the 1861 census of Creemore, there were five Wesleyan Methodists and four Methodist Episcopals. Stephan Lyman, whose family makes up the four, was listed as a Methodist Episcopal minister. By 1871, the numbers had grown to 36 Wesleyan Methodists and 34 Methodist Episcopals. As with the other churches, of course, other members of the congregation came from the rural areas.

WESLEYAN METHODISTS

In the beginning Nottawasaga was one of the outposts of the Mono Mission.[2] Very early in Nottawasaga's settlement, 1838-39, missionary Neelands of Mono "went into the new settlements in the rear of his own circuit."[3]

Again in 1846 there was a report in the Christian Guardian from the Mono missionary, William Glass, "...I send you a brief sketch of the results of a Protracted Meeting held in Nottawasaga township, 4th concession East; commenced December Sunday 28th and continued every evening till January 11th."[4]

Being a missionary in those early days was a difficult occupation. An 1847 report tell of going 35 miles at a time through unbroken forest and inclement weather. On one trip the snow was so deep the man in question had to leave his cutter and go the rest of the way on horseback.[5] In 1856-57 Rev. Hanna reported that going around the Mission requires travel of 250 and 300 miles. In this period Rev. Hanna was responsible for part of Nottawasaga, Osprey, Melancthon, Mulmur and Sunnidale.[6] Even by 1870-71 the area did not get a good report. Rev. James Woodsworth wrote that this area had "some of the worst roads in Canada."[7]

Not only were the travel conditions difficult but the people were also a trial and a tribulation to those courageous travelling missionaries. Wm Glass reported in 1846, "For several years previous to this, these people had not the means of grace among them; their time, especially their Sabbaths, were spent in visiting, cursing, swearing, dancing, fiddling, hunting, and many of them chopping, and sinful practices of almost all kinds."

However, he goes on to say, "How different is the state of things at present, on this part of the line. The Sabbaths are kept holy; their graven images which they worshipped, known by the name of fiddles, are not only laid aside, but burned up. One man on bringing his forward though it cost him when new 21 s sterling, desired me to have it consumed in the flames."[8]

In 1857, there were still problems. "Another year has come to a close; which has been one of toil and trial, in which we were obliged to use the pruning knife of wholesome discipline more frequently than agreeable."[9]

These early missionaries persisted with their efforts. In 1863, a church was erected on Lot 5, Concession 6 of Nottawasaga in an area called Prospect Hill, better known in today's world as Mount Zion.[10] A few years later the Avening community was making plans to build a church.[11] It wasn't until the report for 1872-73 mentioned "the Church in Creemore [that we have] the first definite data which is available concerning a Wesleyan Methodist Church in Creemore," although "the report of 1864-65 indicated a congregation by then."[12]

The church on Caroline Street was later sold and eventually destroyed by fire in 1896.[13] Here there is a difference of opinion. It is reported in the Creemore Star, March 11, 1937, that the church on Caroline Street was the Methodist Episcopal.

METHODIST EPISCOPAL

The research material available for the Methodist Episcopals is not as plentiful as for the Wesleyan Methodists. In 1852 J. Cook and H. Kendrick were preachers for Nottawasaga and St. Vincent Missions. "...[I]n the Barrie Registry Office...Mr. Hiram Kendrick gave some land to 'Joel Underwood, Wm Underwood and James Cook of Nottawasaga Yoeman.' These men are to act as trustees of the land for the Methodist Episcopal Church to be used for a 'cemetery and meeting house.' The land as described in the deed is three quarters of an acre... at the south-east corner of the north-east quarter of lot number 7, concession 5, dated 20th March, 1854."[14]

In the report for 1862 Rev. J. W. McKay was to be stationed in Creemore.[15] Rev. Eagle states that he appears to be the first resident minister of the Methodist Episcopal church in Creemore. However Stephan Lyman is in the 1861 census as Methodist Episcopal and in the 1861 assessment he owns property and is listed as a preacher. The 1865 report lists Rev. P. E. Knox as minister and a membership of 74. The 1870 report tells of a parsonage in Creemore, so it is likely that a church was built previously.[16]

PRIMITIVE METHODISTS

The only material available about the Primitive Methodists is the following tale. "Mr. F. E. Webster used to relate the story about Elijah Wilcox who was, at one time, a member of the Primitive Methodists. They worshipped originally in a small church on the farm now owned by Don Jardine, later they joined the Methodist Episcopal group. Elijah Wilcox in a very fervent prayer, no doubt inspired by a true religious zeal, promised the Lord that if he would come down through the roof that he, Elijah, would pay for having the shingles replaced".[17]

NOTES

1. Methodist Beginnings in Nottawasaga Township (Simcoe County) (Especially as it Relates to the Present Circuit of Creemore).

2. See above, p. 49.

3. Cited p. 50 in Rev. Eagle's book from Carroll's "Case and his Contemporaries 1838-39, p. 191.

4. Cited p. 60 in Rev. Eagle's book from a letter written by Wm Glass in the Christian Guardian, February 11, 1846, p. 65.

5. Cited p. 75 in Rev. Eagle's book from the Christian Guardian,

December 8, 1947, p.30.

6. Rev. Eagle's thesis, pp 98-99.

7. See above, p. 115.

8. Cited in Rev. Eagle's book from a letter by Wm Glass, Christian Guardian, February 11, 1846, p. 65.

9. Cited in Rev. Eagle's book, p. 115 from a report by Rev. James Woodsworth.

10. Rev. Eagle's thesis, p. 107.

11. Cited in Rev. Eagle's book p. 115 from a report by Rev. James Woodsworth.

12. Rev. Eagle's thesis, p. 123.

13. A Glimpse of Creemore's Past, p.73.

14. Rev. Eagle's thesis, pp 136-137.

15. See above, p. 144.

16. See above, p. 148.

17. The Centennial History of St. John's United Church, Creemore, Ontario, 1886-1986.

THE BAPTIST CHURCH

The Baptists in Creemore were also divided along theological beliefs. A study of Baptist history in Canada reveals their differences and tells of the hardships encountered similar to the other churches. The first quote that follows was written by Mrs. H. E. Fraser, a long time member of the Creemore church.

"In the early days of Nottawasaga township theological students from Woodstock College spent summers preaching and gathering together worshippers of the Baptist faith. These students travelled on foot or possibly in some cases on horseback. They were entertained in homes throughout the area and preached in schools or other unused buildings. Eventually they had five preaching stations in the "Nottawasaga Field" and up to 1866 Creemore was one of them. Rev. Alex McIntyre came as the first Baptist minister in the township and remained until 1869.

The Canadian Baptist Register, of a century ago, has this to say concerning the work at Creemore: 'Mr. McIntyre preaches in Gaelic and in English. A chapel erected in the summer was dedicated on Dec. 26, 1869. The Home Mission Secretary visited this field and was greatly gratified by what he saw and heard. Mr. McIntyre is doing a great work, and the aspect on the field is greatly changed for the better during the year.'"

The Creemore church which was first a small frame chapel was located on Collingwood St."[1] This frame building had a seating capacity of 100 and was on the east side of Collingwood Street just to the north of Francis Street.[2]

For quite a number of years the Creemore church was affiliated with Stayner. The following figures are somewhat meaningless because the Baptists from around the country would come to the village but they indicate the general population of the religion. In the 1871 census of Creemore there were 16 Baptists and that is counting young children. Four were regular Baptists and twelve were Christian Conference Baptists. This seems hardly enough to start a church. However, as the church was established by 1867 there must have been enough active and interested members.

The small group of this particular religion is not surprising. It has been written, "[I]n 1815 if anyone had taken a poll on the future of the Baptist cause in Upper Canada the opinion registered would have been 'without hope.'" [3] The Baptist Church was much more active in the Maritimes. The church did grow but the number of ministers did not keep up. It was reported in 1846 that there were only half as many ordained men as churches.[4]

Stayner seems to have been among the fortunate half to have had a minister. Their church was begun in 1854, and by 1866 the Rev. Alex McIntyre, mentioned previously, was making the journey to Creemore to meet the spiritual needs of Creemore Baptists. With our modern roads it is hard to appreciate the difficulties in a trip from Stayner to Creemore. Spring mud and winter storms would be among the hazards. From 1869-72, Rev. Alex Warren was in charge.[5]

The different persuasions of Baptists came together in 1889 calling themselves the Baptist Convention. The main difference, it seems, between the two mentioned above is that the Christian Conference Baptists favoured Open Communion, that is, anyone who was a Christian could partake, but the Regular Baptists felt that only baptized Baptists could participate in communion in their church.[6] Obviously the two groups in Creemore resolved their differences and came together to form the one church.

The congregation became stronger and the church flourished but that is a story for later.

NOTES

1. This account of the early days of the Baptist church in Creemore was written by Mrs. H.E. Fraser and appeared in The Canadian Baptist, September 1, 1967, pp. 1 & 3.
   2. Creemore Star, March 11, 1937, p. 2.
   3. Heritage and Horizons: The Baptist Story in Canada, p.71.
   4. See above, p. 94.
   5. 140th Anniversary of First Baptist, Stayner.
6. Ken Morgan, Archivist, Canadian Baptist Archives, Hamilton, Ontario, telephone interview, April 22, 1999.

THE CATHOLIC CHURCH

A group of Irish Catholics found land and built homes and farms on the Fourth Line north of Creemore. They established a Catholic congregation and soon after built a church. There was no Catholic Church in Creemore so it may be assumed that those of that faith made their way up the hill to the area commonly known as Bayview. In the 1861 census there were 10 Catholics listed in Creemore and in the 1871 census this had fallen to three.

The following account has been carefully researched and written by Agnes J. Douglas, nee Giffen, of Collingwood who very kindly has given permission to use it.

Most of the pioneers in this area [that is, at Bayview] were devoted Roman Catholics and had no intention of neglecting their religious duties or the education of their children. The first visit of a priest to the neighbourhood of the now Stayner area was Fr. Proux accompanied by an Indian Chief, crossing the Nottawasaga River on a raft and opened an Indian Mission where no white man had yet settled. The location is uncertain. The next visit was in January 1839 by the Pastor of Adjala, Fr. Fitzpatrick. This mass was said in a lumber shanty belonging to John Bertles at Duntroon. This information was passed on from "Jubilee Volume Archbishop Walsh" and came from St. Mary's Church, Barrie, Ontario.

Father Charest of Penetanguishine had formal charge of this district and Mass was celebrated once a year for four years, then twice a year in the Dowling log barn to attend to the spiritual wants of those faithful settlers scattered throughout the great forest in Nottawasaga and other townships far and near.

Some of the missionaries' names that came to say Mass were Fathers: Cherrier, Lee, Northgraves, O'Connor and Synnet from 1840 to 1848 in the barn and then in the log church after it was built on a 1-acre site in the northeast corner of the Dowling property in 1848. [The site for this church may be seen today where there is a little cemetery on the west side of the Fourth Line.] The church was built under the leadership of John Bertles, Matthew Dowling, Edmund Duggan and a mechanic, Patrick McKeown. As roads opened up, Mass was also celebrated at other locations such as Lawlor's Farm near the Devil's Glen and at William Fenlon's Farm directly across the road from the present St. Patrick's Cemetery on Highway 91 then called Bowmore Road. This was after roads were made and travelling was much easier than the long tramps by foot these courageous missionaries endured long before Barrie, Stayner, or Collingwood parishes were even started. By now the missionaries were travelling by horseback which was impossible when they had only an Indian trail to follow through the forest. They would stay in the community long enough to rest before attempting that long journey home to Penetanguishine.

One incident told about a priest that was so overcome with exhaustion that he collapsed on the floor of the Dowling residence and he lay for hours without being aware of where he was or how long he had slept. In the meantime, Bridget Dowling removed his boots and socks, bathed and treated his blistered feet, and washed and darned his socks before he woke up. Such hardships were not new to these travelling missionaries that were made welcome in the Dowling home. There were many duties for the priests to perform, not the least of these was Baptism. Parents were not blessed with the opportunity to have their children baptised as infants because of the long distance they must carry the child and other children unable to walk that far. It was not unusual for them to be near school age before receiving the Sacrament or for two or three children from the same family to receive it at one time.

This particular story was told many times over the years, in a very colourful manner, of a beautiful early summer day when one of the Priests celebrated Mass in the barn and baptized the children of the large crowd of pioneers that had congregated to worship. It was great fun for the children to meet other children for the first time, to run and play and receive a few scrapes and bloodly noses as well. It was impossible to keep the children separated long enough for them to be baptized, so as a result some of them were being missed or lost until someone got the idea of herding them into the animal pens in the stable and letting them out in turns. Then they were put in another pen after they had received the Sacrament. This served the purpose very well except that the fist fights became most intense in the small areas. There were many adults ready and willing to act as godparents. However, at the end of the day they were not quite sure how many or just whom they had stood for.

Constructing log buildings was a major project which took many man hours from the cutting of the trees to the final finished timbers suitable for building. All of this was necessary for a home and shelter for the farm stock and fodder, which, little by little, the settlers had acquired.

The building of a log church was quite another matter! It was built out of love and devotion to the faith that no amount of hardship could shatter. Many willing workers, that were in the habit of attending Mass in the barn, donated their labour in the preparation of the construction of the little church. They now had a church, a separate school and a cemetery and they were justly proud of their achievement. According to the Simcoe County Registry Office, a deed registration was signed on March 2, 1858 by Matthew Dowling and the Roman Catholic Episcopal Corporation. Also a deed dated December 1, 1863 for the above, from the same as the above, for the northeast corner of Lot 13, Concession 5, 1-acre in the Township of Nottawasaga for the church and cemetery.

It is interesting to note the church was built ten years before the deeds were registered. This delay is also seen pertaining to the farm which leaves such dates in question in early years.[1]

NOTES
1. The Dowling Family History and the History of the First Roman Catholic Church and the First Separate School in Nottawasaga Township, pp. 4-6.

THE CEMETERY

It is possible that you have begun to read this with the idea that you will learn the early history of Creemore's cemetery. You will probably end up more confused than enlightened. That is because there is conflicting information and very little solid evidence to support any of it. There follows an explanation of the problems.

In a little booklet produced by the Cemetery Board in 1985 it states that the land was granted by the Crown to the Church of England about 1840. However, research indicates that in 1840 it did not belong to the Crown. It had been granted to Maria Robertson in 1836 by the Crown under the scheme of grants to United Empire Loyalists or veterans of the War of 1812-14.[1] In this case Maria Robertson was likely a descendant of one of them. It would also seem unlikely that a plot of land would be granted to an area that didn't have anyone living nearby. Creemore wasn't even in anyone's wildest dreams at that time.

In the Anglican Church centennial history, 100 Years of History: St. Luke's, Creemore, it states, "Mr. Edward Webster donated a site for a Church and Cemetery.[2] Mr. Webster's first wife, Elizabeth Ann, who died in 1853 following childbirth, was the first burial made in the newly established cemetery." At this point we have the most solid piece of information that would give us a clue as to when the land became available for the cemetery. In the land records on Sept. 11, 1849, Edward Webster etux of Nottawasaga, gave to John Lord Bishop of Toronto pt. of 1 acre in Lot 8, Concession 4, no consideration (i.e. money) indicated.[3] A little comma can be of the utmost importance. The words, "John Lord Bishop of Toronto," indicate that the man's name was John Lord Bishop and he lived in Toronto. If a comma were to be inserted, as in "John Lord, Bishop of Toronto" the meaning changes. This would seem to indicate that the Bishop of Toronto received the land for the Church of England.

The statement that Elizabeth Ann Webster was the first burial in the 'newly' established cemetery also leads one astray. In 1853 it was hardly new if established in 1849. The Creemore Cemetery index lists several burials before 1853. These were Jane Corbitt, May 21, 1851; Nancy Jane Porter, April 12, 1850; Henry Boyes, June 1, 1851; and William Arthur Spacey, Jan. 21. 1851. On the Leach family stone are listed Charles,

Sept. 13, 1847 and William, Sept. 20, 1849. In the latter case the parents are also listed at a later date, and possibly Charles and William are listed as a memorial only.[4] The unfortunate reality for the pioneers was that burials had to be made on the individual's property if a cemetery was not available. This caused much heartache as people preferred a sacred piece of ground where the burial would not be forgotten.

The Creemore Cemetery books, now in the possession of Jim Steed, Creemore, do not exist for that early year. The Creemore Anglican Church records have recently and wisely been placed in the hands of the Anglican Church Archives in Toronto. There is nothing there to indicate what year the cemetery was established. There are no assessment records before 1858, either, so our guess that the cemetery land was turned over in 1849 relies on the transfer to John Lord, Bishop of Toronto in the land records.

NOTES
    1. Land records for Lot 8, Concession 4, Nottawasaga, seen at the Land Registry Office, Barrie.
    2. 100 Years of History: St. Luke's Church, Creemore, p. 2.
    3. Land records for Lot 8, Concession 4, Nottawasaga.
    4. Corbitt, #950; Porter, #994; Boyes, #996; Spacey, #1011; Leach, #1064 in the Creemore Union Cemetery Index.

IF THERE HAD BEEN A CREEMORE NEWSPAPER

If Creemore had had a newspaper when it was in its infancy these might be the news items reported. Some are written in retrospect, others are written as they were when the event occurred.

HOW THE MAD RIVER RECEIVED ITS NAME[1]

Rev. Father Jeffcott, pastor of St. Patrick's Church, Stayner, while visiting his parishioners in Nottawasaga, was told of an interesting incident of early life in the township, on account of which it is said the Mad River received its name.

In the year 1835 Mrs. Matt Dowling of the 4th line, who celebrated her 89th birthday on May 1st, and who is probably the oldest living inhabitant of Nottawasaga, was one day returning home carrying on her back a sack of flour which she was bringing from a distant mill. In addition to the flour she had in her arms her eldest child and laden in this manner she forded the river at the site of the present Glen Huron. The stream was running turbulently. She had great difficulty in winning her way across and no doubt had she not possessed the strength of the sturdy pioneers of those rugged days she would have ended her experience then and there.

When Mrs. Dowling reached home she was considerably excited and in telling of her adventure she referred repeatedly to "that mad river," in which she had nearly drowned. And from that day the stream that runs down from the Osprey hills and rushes noisily through Creemore has been known as the Mad river.

A MURDER IN CREEMORE[2]

It is not often we are called upon to record man shooting [sic] in Canada, but we are informed of a most painful occurrence of the kind, that occurred on Monday last. The quiet village of Creemore was thrown into a great state of excitement early on that day, by what is feared will prove fatal to the life of an industrious young man, by the name of William Hogg, a Shoemaker, residing in the Village. It appears young Hogg had been at variance with his Step-father, John Salter, also living near, for a considerable time past, respecting a right or property, and on the morning in question, after some altercation in words, the old man walked into his house and returned with a loaded pistol, and deliberately placing it to the left side of the young man, fired, the ball passing under the ribs to the backbone where it lodged. He was instantly removed to a tavern close by, where a magistrate, E. Webster, Esq., was sent for, who with other assistance, proceeded towards the house of Salter to arrest him. Salter, seeing this, came out to meet them and quietly yielded himself as prisoner into their hands. He is now in Barrie Gaol.

The ball has been extracted, but the young man is not expected to recover. The painful affair has spread a gloom over the neighbourhood, where both parties were respected as honest and industrious neighbours. The unfortunate prisoner is over 70 years of age.

The following information has been added in <u>A Glimpse of Creemore's Past</u>. "According to local lore, Mr. Salter and Mr. Hogg had a dispute over some work they were doing with a pair of boots and the shooting was the result of their quarrel. Another story was told that Hogg had a weakness for drinking whiskey. In one of his drunken brawls, he became very abusive to his mother, and this was why Salter shot him. Be that as it may, the young Mr. Hogg died from his wounds and Mr. Salter paid the penalty for his crime by receiving capital punishment."[3]

A further comment: No evidence of the trial appears in the bench notes of the Simcoe County judges of the time, nor is there any report in the Barrie newspapers for two years following the murder.

William Hogg is buried in Creemore Cemetery. The inscription on his stone says, "William Hogg, died July 13, 1857, aged 20 years and 11 days."[4]

THE BATTLE OF BOWMORE

Taken from Reminiscences by F. T. Hodgson which was published in <u>The Collingwood Enterprise, 1907</u>.[5]

Somewhere about the winter of 1853 or '54, at the Township Meeting held at the corners [Bowmore, now Duntroon], an event occurred that I can never forget. It was a beautiful winter's day and the gathering was from all parts of the township, particularly from Creemore and the 4th and 6th lines. There had always been rivalry between the Highland Scotch element and the Irish, good natured it was, but both sides loved a bit of a scuffle when too well primed with whiskey. On this occasion, before the polls closed a race was proposed by some of the men, between an Irish and a Scotch champion. The two competitors chosen were Sandy

Kerr for the Irish, and Sandy Campbell for the Scotch. Both these young fellows were braced up with plenteous drafts of good malt whiskey. The crowd gathered. The course was measured, and with a one, two, three, they were started. Neither of the racers could run in a straight line, and before the goal was reached they had covered considerably more than the measured distance. Eventually they finished so close together that it was difficult to know which was the victor. A dispute arose instantly. All took sides and in less than 10 minutes, every man was fast locked in a grapple with his nearest foe. There were no police to maintain order and it was the biggest row known. I always called it the battle of Bowmore. The fight extended over two hours till sundown and the combatants swayed to and fro off the hard road into the deep snow, each too drunk to do his enemy any harm. I sat with several other boys on a fence outside Willing's Hotel and cheered them on. Darkness fell ere the battle ceased and an old Irishman named McBride...took a lantern and went to seek for the dead and wounded, finding none, he searched carefully for traces of blood, but in vain. The battle of Bowmore was therefore unlike that of Linden "when the sun was low." To this day, no decision of this memorable race has been satisfactorily given.

1855 NOTTAWASAGA ELECTION

This bit of news from our area appeared in the Barrie, <u>Northern Advance,</u> January 17, 1855.[6]

Letter from Bibliopola, Nottawasaga, January 4, 1855, re election.

J. D. Stephens	170
Richard Madill	148
C. Campbell	142
Peter Ferguson	123
Francis Kerr	113

The election was conducted, as far as I saw and heard, in a perfectly orderly manner. There was neither fighting nor drunkenness among the people which is more than can be said of other meetings throughout Canada, or I am greatly mistaken. In fact, the great mass of inhabitants of this Township who have formerly been addicted to excessive drinking are beginning to see the evil of such practices

A PORT AT THE MOUTH OF THE BATTEAUX CREEK

It used to be that when local people had a complaint or a problem the only recourse was a petition to a government official many miles away, in this case, Quebec. A group of early pioneers in the Creemore area began thinking that it would be an advantage to have a port at the north end of the Fourth Line or near the mouth of the Batteaux Creek. Supplies in 1853 had to be transported over a tortuous route from Barrie. Having it arrive by water at the mouth of the Batteaux would simplify things they reasoned. They got together and composed a petition to Honorable John Rolfe, Commissioner for Crown Lands, Quebec. They gave evidence of the growth in the area and their reasons for this port. Then someone canvassed the Fourth Line residents for signatures. The following list is from the Creemore area.

Edward Webster	Lot 8, con.	4.
Hiram Kendrick	7	5
George Webster	8	4
W. Kelly	8	4
James Shields	7	5
John Kendrick	8	4
J. [W]init	7	4
George [W]init	7	4
Wm Leonard	7	4
George Foster	8	5
Wm Casie	8	5[7]

NO MAN'S LAND

The following petitions tell the story of a piece of land that somehow got missed when the surveyors were laying out the townships.

Creemore Mills 17 Dec. 1852

To The Honourable John Ralph Com. Of Crown Lands Quebec

Sir:

I have the honour to enclose a certificate from a Senior Surveyor of Lot 33 in 1st Con East half of Tosorontio now in the new survey lately made by Mr. H. P. Savigney that I have been prepared to improve upon this Lot and commenced working upon it some 18 months back but have found out that it was not attached to either Township, unsurveyed and not for sale. I was afraid to go on with improvements till I secured the title. I have the honour to request that I may be allowed to purchase and shall be thankful for an answer as soon as possible as I want to make arrangements this winter for improving upon it.

I have the honour to be Sirs

E. Webster

The letter from the surveyor.

This is to certify that the improvements to lot 33 in the 1st of Tosorontio were made for Edward Webster by his brother George Webster and a hired man James Wait about the 8th Sept 1851 and on finding that the lot was in the Gore. W. Webster [sic] would not proceed till he had the sanction of the Government. They underbrushed and partly chopped [unclear] and cut house logs. There is no claim out to the lot and no settlers within 3 miles by the new road made by Mr. Webster at his own expense and in my opinion Mr. Webster is entitled to great consideration from the Government for the improvement he has made (especially in regards to roads) in Nottawasaga and surrounding townships. I have the honour to remain

Sir

Your most obedient S't

Wm Gibbard PLS[8]

NOTES

1. Creemore Star, May 14, 1903, p. 4.
2. Northern Advance, Barrie, Thursday, July 23,1857, as cited in A Glimpse of Creemore's Past, p. 26.
3. A Glimpse of Creemore's Past, p. 26.
4. Creemore Union Cemetery Index, #1133.
5. Nottawasaga: The Outburst of the Iroquois, pp. 64-65.
6. Northern Advance, Barrie, January 17, 1855, p.3., c. 1.
7. On file at the Simcoe County Archives, Midhurst.
8. Land Petitions W 7/6, Vol. 542, Archives of Ontario.

FIRST FAMILIES

Many of the very first families to live in Creemore and close by have descendants still in the village and on property nearby. Large families were the ideal in pioneer days and most of the children, when young adults, moved on to far away fields that looked greener. We have here six of those early families. For each family there is only a brief sketch, naming the first generation, telling where so many wandered and mentioning some of the present day descendants. There are other important local families worthy of a write-up and they may be included in another book.

THE GALLOWAY FAMILY

Although there are no people by the name of Galloway in Creemore today, some descendants are very much in our midst.[1] Henry Galloway, Carpenter, and Thomas Galloway, Shoemaker, may be found in the early assessments. They are not, however, listed in the census returns. This means they owned property in the village but lived somewhere outside of it.

The story of the Galloways goes back to Fermanagh, Ireland.[2] James Galloway, along with Yonges, Hoggs, and Pinkertons arrived in Canada some years before 1837. He settled first north of Muddy York at Hogg's Hollow, afterwards called York Mills. A little later he bought land at what was then called Pinkerton's Corners, four miles south and two miles east of the village of Cookstown. He married Ann Pinkerton. According to the family records which Joan Wilson has researched, the two were married in Ireland.[3] They had thirteen children.

James Galloway was at one time the miller of the Old Mill on the Humber River. Having learned milling in Ireland before coming to Canada he applied for and got the position of operator of this stone mill. It was at this work that he was killed in the spring of 1838 by the bursting of a millstone. He was buried in the old cemetery at the church on top of the hill at York Mills where many of his pioneer friends are also buried.

Now jumping ahead to 1903 the story goes on. Samuel Galloway, who was then living in Creemore, decided to visit his daughter in Toronto. He started from Creemore on the morning train and landed at his daughter's home, safe and sound. He was then 81 years of age. After he had eaten his dinner he asked his daughter to take him to the Old Mill on the Humber. While there he described to her how he and his mother had driven a yoke of oxen and a sleigh with five bags of wheat on it all the way from the farm near Cookstown to this mill to be ground into flour. He showed his daughter where the office had been and where the millstones were located when he, as a boy, had made the trip to Cookstown to the mill where his father worked.

There is no record at present of when some of the Galloways came to the Creemore area. Several of the brothers were in the area and the mother, then a widow, is said to have come to Creemore to work for Honeyfords.[4] She died August 30, 1861, age 59 years and is buried in Creemore Cemetery.[5]

It is recorded that "[t]he first celebration of the Battle of the Boyne held in the township [Nottawasaga]...was about 1850 and took place at the Galloway homestead, where Bayview school now stands. Two lodges, "Bowmore," later called Duntroon, and Tory Hill [Purple Hill] were present. Mr. Galloway, proud of the honor done him by having so many guests, had dinner provided for every one."[6] This quote has produced some small mysteries. Thanks to the sharp eyes of Joan Wilson it was realized that Joseph Galloway who had a farm near Bayview was only 12 or 13 at the time, hardly likely to host a 12th of July. A check into the 1858 Assessment of Nottawasaga brought some answers. Yes, Joseph Galloway did live on the sideroad near Bayview and lived there for quite a few years so that his farm is the one automatically thought of at Bayview. The assessment records, however, list five Galloways in Nottawasaga. Matthew Galloway, a tailor, 22, was on a one acre lot, SW part lot 13, concession 4. James Galloway, 34, was on the west half of lot 13, concession 4. Joseph Galloway, 21, had the E half of lot 13, concession 4. David Galloway was on lot 13, concession 2, and Henry Galloway was a carpenter, 30, 1/4 acre, lot 8, concession 5.

So it would have been James Galloway who hosted the 12th of July celebration as he was on the west part of lot 13 and that is right at Bayview, the north-east corner. Now, about the school. The one we recognize is on the south-east corner. Agnes Douglas, who knows a great deal about Bayview, has stated that the original Protestant school was on the north-east corner.[7] So that was the school referred to in the 1934 history of Nottawasaga quoted above.

Previously mentioned was the fact that James and Ann Galloway had thirteen children and when all the grandchildren are noted it adds up to 111 of them. And it is also to be noted that son, Henry, remained a bachelor. Not all of the family came to Creemore but it is known that Jane married Lachlan Adair and there are Adair descendants in the Creemore area. Nancy Galloway married John Davis and of their descendants you will recognize the names Bill Timmons and Dorothy Shropshire. Samuel married Fanny McCausland and from the above anecdote, was living in Creemore in 1903. Thomas Galloway married Caroline Manning. Although the Manning name has disappeared there are currently relatives around.

Joseph married Eliza Williams and their family has many local descendants. One daughter, Elizabeth married a Lawrence. Levina married Tom Miller. Annie married Oswald Jardine. Clementine married Fred Steele. Wilhelmina married James Agar. Jenny married Albert Adams. Their daughter, Eliza Millsap, is one of our eldest citizens. A son, Everett went out west.

There was a Galloway photography studio on King Street in Creemore for a few years after 1900. A small building at the back of a house on that street had windows in the roof and at the side for proper lighting.

So many children! So many grandchildren! Where did they all go? Some of the family went to Pilot Mound, Manitoba, but little else is presently known about the rest of the family.

NOTES
1. Thanks goes to Bill Timmons, Joan Wilson and Elsie Agar for the information they shared about the Galloways.
2. This information is from the Genealogical and Historical Records of the Davis and Galloway Families, 1822-1947.
3. Joan Wilson, Stayner, interview June 1999.
4. Joan Wilson, June, 1999.
5. Creemore Cemetery index. Other Galloway names may be found in the same publication.
6. Nottawasaga: The Outburst of the Iroquois, p. 11.
7. The school location confirmed by Agnes Douglas, Collingwood, June 1999.

THE GIFFEN FAMILY [1]

The name of Giffen is well known in Creemore. No one by that name lives in the village of Creemore to-day but families by that name have been in the vicinity since our area's earliest days.

Andrew Giffen was one of the earliest settlers in Creemore. He was born in Kilbarkan, Scotland, not far from the city of Paisley. He was the son of James Giffen and Margaret Millar. Andrew's brother, Robert, came to Canada in 1842 and found work in Chinguacousy Township, Peel County. Andrew came a bit later.[2] It is not certain exactly when he made his way to Creemore. Andrew, his wife and young family were among the earliest residents of Creemore. As previously mentioned, it was thought they owned the land that became the Creemore village site but no official record appears to exist.

There also appears to be a difference of opinion over Andrew's son, William, being the first child born in Creemore. According to family records and cemetery recordings he was born in 1855. Already in 1855 there were families with children born in the village. Perhaps at one time someone got confused about his birthdate and thought 1845 for 1855. If he had been born in 1845 he would have been the first child born in Creemore.

Andrew, after a short time in Creemore, left the village for a more favourable farming site on Lot 18, Concession 6 in Nottawasaga. Andrew had married Agnes Forbes and they had children, William, Robert, Andrew, Margaret, Martha, Lizzie and James. When James was a little boy he lost his life by drowning in the Mad River at Creemore. Agnes died in 1863 and is buried at Creemore. Andrew was married a second time to Esther Henning and had seven more children. Unfortunately, no one seems to know anything about the history of this second family, only that one son, John, was killed by a train at Smithdale.

A note here for readers who don't know where Smithdale is. It is at the corner of the Sixth Line and Sideroad 18/19, Nottawasaga. Although a very quiet little burg at the present time it was once a bustling little town as the following account indicates.

"The building of the railroad through the township in the late eighties created quite a boom in the areas adjacent to the railway right-of-way. Mr. Giffen was getting on in years, at all events he handed over the management of the farm to members of his family and he built a hotel and large rooming house at a location near the site of what eventually became Glen Huron station.

The contractors establishing the grade in preparation for the laying of steel maintained a temporary headquarters building. There were a few private buildings erected including a blacksmith shop where several men were employed. This is understandable because many teams of horses were used in the work of establishing the grade and work horses must be kept shod.

This site was the hub of plenty of activity and Giffen's Hotel was the popular site. My grandfather [Bert Smith's] had donated the land for the station site. Part of the agreement the land purchasers made with my grandfather was that the government would survey a village site on a field adjacent to where the station would be built. The surveyors did their job and to maintain the good-will the company decided to call the centre Smithville. The village site was registered at the County Register office in Barrie and the name Smithville may be found on early township maps. Grandfather was to benefit by any sale of lots. If he entertained any expectations of capital gain they soon faded because the entire centre quickly folded after the building of the railroad.

Andrew Giffen was regarded as the leading citizen of this busy centre, but, when he heard the company had officially named the place "Smithville" he was disgusted. He didn't like the name and he felt slighted that he had not been consulted. He recalled Kilbarkan as the name of a town in his native Scotland and he decreed it to be the name of this village. The name caught on and many used it for a number of years.

The community decided to petition for a post office. The petition was granted but when the post office department found out there already was a village near Hamilton named Smithville, they said the post office would be known as Smithdale. In the meantime, Andrew Giffen had died, otherwise there is no doubt that he would have insisted on it being called Kilbarkan."[3]

Now let us go back to William Giffen's family. He married Mary

Dowling Malone, the same Mary who was carried by her mother the day the Mad River was named. They had sons, James Peter and Robert Andrew. James Peter's son, Bill, who recently passed away was well known in Creemore, particularly at the Legion. Bill had four sisters, Kathleen, Helen, Agnes and Anna. Son, Murray, lived on the original Dowling farm, but has moved to Collingwood.

William and Mary's second son, Robert Andrew married Gertrude Madden and they had children Mary, Margaret, Frank, Irene, Robert and Martina. You will recognize Frank Giffen's name as the industrious farmer who established a fruit and poultry business at Glen Huron. Frank lost his life in a farm accident in 1976, but his family have continued to carry on in a most successful manner.

Like many families, the Giffens chose to use certain names over and over. There were many Roberts. This particular Robert is one of Andrew's sons. Robert died in 1917, his early death attributed to his hard work overcoming adverse times. His obituary[4] tells us he was a Nottawasaga councillor from 1911 to the time of his death. His family consisted of Jennie, Robert, Bertha and Peter N. Peter N. was a well-known farmer on the Fourth Line north of Creemore. Although some of his habits are the subject of local legend, he was highly regarded for his intelligence and financial acumen.

Back to the first Andrew again. A son moved to Manitoba and daughters to Michigan, Cookstown and Toronto.

Fortunately Andrew has had his name forever inscribed in local history for there is no account of his death. When did he die? Where is he buried? Does he have a marker with his name engraved far all to remember as they pass?

NOTES
1. Eileen Giffen of Glen Huron and Agnes Douglas of Collingwood provided much assistance in putting together this account of the Giffens.
2. The Giffen History from 1842-1970.
3. From "A Man Called Giffen" in the 1867 booklet, Centennial Stories of Creemore, Nottawasaga, Their People, a collection of Anecdotes, Family Histories and some selections of the Writing of C.B. Smith, pp. 75-76.
4. Collingwood Saturday News, August 4, 1917, p. 2, c. 1.

THE GOWAN FAMILY

Enough could be said about the Gowan family to fill another book but due to space restrictions this account will have to be a brief outline. Frank Webster, whose mother was Esther Gowan, began in his old age to record the Gowan family tree. Alice Emmett, continued his work. As yet, however, the information is in a rough format. A world wide history of the Gowans was printed in 1978. A copy is in the Creemore Library.[1]

In Mr. Webster's shaky handwriting on now yellowing paper are the words, "William Gowan 1797-1846 and wife Ann Pillsworth emigrated from Nock Bond, market Town, Maryborough, Queen's County, Ireland in the year 1846 and their family of 11 children. All arrived in good health and grew to manhood and womanhood and married and led a family life. 83 children were born to these families."

Mount Rath has also been identified as their home in Ireland. The name of County Queens was changed to Laois (pronounced Leesh) after the south and north of Ireland separated. Nock Bond is probably Knockbawn. The year of arrival in Canada is confusing. If William died in 1846, then they must have come here in 1845, or else they came in 1846 and he died in 1847.

The eleven children were Jane, Francis, Mary Ann, Lizzie (or Elizabeth), Sam, Essey (or Esther), Charlotte, Tom, William, Margaret and Susan (or Susannah).

Another source, identity unknown, states, "They came with a family of eleven to the district of Bond Head. Shortly after arrival the children took sick with typhus and great grandfather [William] nursed them through this illness, later to succumb to the disease himself."

William is buried in the Middletown cemetery near Bond Head in Simcoe County. On William's stone is written, "To the memory of William Gowan who died Feb. 2, 1846, 48 years 11 months. Born near Mt. Rath, Ireland." His wife, Ann, lived to age 74, died in 1874 in Creemore and is buried in Creemore cemetery.

How the family survived after the breadwinner was gone has never been explained. The older ones were old enough to go out in the neighbourhood and work. The family did survive and flourish and their many descendants populate the Creemore area. As well, many are scattered across the North American continent.

The eldest, Jane, married John Hare soon after they arrived in Canada. John was a hotel keeper at Rosemont. Later he was a pioneer farmer on lot 27, concession 8 in Mulmur. Their family consisted of William, Frederick, Sarah Jane, Robert, Annie, Samuel and Mary. The Hare name is well known in Creemore. Other names associated with this family are Prosser, Falls, Penelton and Jones. Sarah Jane married William McNall. Their son, Thomas, went west in 1909, bought out the Weston biscuit business in Regina and served as mayor and alderman in that city for 18 years.

Francis Gowan married Mary Jane Manning. He was a pioneer farmer on lot 5, concession 5, Nottawasaga and had a family of ten: William, Maria, Belinda, Charlotte, Thomas, John, Francis, Annie, Mary and Samuel. Samuel's son, Carl, and family, were the last of the family to live on the pioneer homestead. Other local names associated with this family are Cooksey, Perry, Branch, Gallaugher, and McMullen. Creemore's park is named for Carl Gowan as a tribute to his contribution to sports in Creemore, and it seems, as well, to the Gowan legacy of fine athletes.

Mary Ann married John Carlton. She was John's second wife but he died in 1868 leaving her with four young children. One of them, Mary, was a teacher at Creemore school for many years. The eldest son, Francis, better known as F. S., went to Sault Ste Marie where he established a thriving hardware business. He later moved on to the Keneewaw Peninsula in Upper Michigan where his hardware business grew even larger as he supplied the copper mining area. This store is still in existence, and while no longer in the Carlton name, it is still a huge, busy operation.

Elizabeth married Levi Rogers, a man with a Quaker background. A descendant, Bill Rogers, lived in Websterville until he moved to Toronto. Many of the Roger descendants are in Saskatchewan.

Samuel Gowan was married to Ann Kenny, was a blacksmith in many places but spent most of his life at Banda.

Esther married George Webster. More information about this family is under the Webster name.

Thomas, who married Elizabeth Martin, was a carpenter, later a storekeeper in Creemore and still later went to Sault Ste Marie, Michigan. Two of his sons went to the Cuban War and only one came back.

Charlotte married her first cousin, Colclough Gowan, (usually pronounced Cokely). Colclough was a mason, travelled around the world and farmed on lot 1, concession 6, Nottawasaga. A son was a dentist in Creemore for awhile. One of Charlotte's and Colclough's descendants was a Rhodes Scholar. This couple retired to Creemore.

William married Kathleen Wright and is best remembered for his hotel in Creemore, known as Gowan's Tavern or the Traveller's Inn. An ad in an old Gazeteer says, "William Gowan, proprietor Traveller's Inn. This house is pleasantly situated and affords every accommodation. The best brands of Wines, Liquors, and Cigars. Good Stabling. N. B. The vicinity is unequalled for trout fishing."[2]

In 1870 he opened another hotel in Singhampton and finally another one in Alliston where he died under strange circumstances that have never been fully explained. It is explained here in the words of his granddaughter, Miriam Fraser. "My father's sisters, Aunt Mae Gowan Hotton and Aunt Dolly Gowan Roach would have answered [questions] if I had asked as a child. My father never talked about his father in my hearing. So I asked Mom what happened to Grandpa Gowan. And she answered me, rather formally, that she had been told that Grandpa Gowan had been taking external medicine for lumbago, and internal medicine for a severe cold, and that he had taken the wrong medicine internally, which led to his death. This was when my Dad was twelve years old, c. 1888. So Grandpa William is buried probably in an Anglican cemetery in your area."[3] His family went to Sault Ste Marie and the descendants are scattered all over the United States.

Margaret married Richard Irwin, a pioneer farmer, lot 3, concession 3, Mulmur. They retired in Alliston. Many of his family went to Saskatchewan but Dr. John Irwin was a dentist in Collingwood.

Susan married Robert Irvine who was an artist, painter, contractor, etc. and lived at Orangeville.

Many names in the Creemore phone book tell of the Gowan descendants. They are: C. Gowan, Carman Gowan, Dan Gowan, E. Gowan, Gertrude Gowan, Rick Gowan, T. Gowan and W. F. Gowan.

NOTES
1. The Genealogy of the Clan Gowan.
2. Gazeteer and Directory of the county of Simcoe for 1866-67.
3. Letter from Miriam Fraser, February 11, 1996, Ventura, CA.

THE SIDEY FAMILY

Among the land owners in the 1866 Assessment of Creemore is James Sidey, whose descendants are still in the area in 1999. At that time he was listed as owning property on Caroline and Laura Streets. He is also listed in the 1871 census but just on the outskirts of the village. On an 1871 map of Nottawasaga his name is on the west half of Lot 9, Concession 5.[1]

We do not know anything at this point about James Sidey's life before he came to Creemore. The 1871 Census tells us he was 34 years old and that he was born in Ontario but of Scotch background.[2] One of his great grandsons, Winton Schneider of Collingwood, was able to add some more information about his family. Winton came from Alberta in the midst of the Great Depression to Creemore and lived with his Uncle Bill Sidey and Aunt Mina while going to high school in the village.

James was married to Cordelia Grace, known by her second name of Grace. Their children were Kate, John, Mary, George, Albert, William, Richard, Louisa and Bessie. As a coincidence, four of the daughters married men believed to be of German descent. Kate married a Rumbough. She lived in Gananoque. Mary married a Schneider and they lived in Alberta. Louisa married a Klopp and Bessie a Haight, and both are believed to have lived in Toronto.

Son, John, farmed west of Creemore just beyond the fringes of Websterville. Bill had the farm at the far end of Caroline Street, Creemore, just as the road turns south to Mount Zion and Richard had a farm behind that. Albert was a bachelor and for a time had a farm in Sunnidale Township. The latter years of his life were spent with his brother, John. George lived part of his life on Manitoulin Island.

Richard lost his life tragically in 1916. A Creemore Star article tells the tale.[3] "A sad accident, which resulted in fatality, occurred on Wednesday morning last week at 11 o'clock on the farm of Willoughby Nesbitt, a short distance from town. A barn purchased by Richard Sidey was being torn down and moved to his farm where he intended rebuilding. In the course of operations while the men were standing on the barn floor, suddenly, and without warning, one of the beams loosened, no doubt by decayed supports, and fell a distance of twenty feet, striking Mr. Sidey on the head with such force as to render him unconscious. At first it was thought that he had been killed, but a few moments later showed signs of life. Dr. Bradley was called and he was removed to the home of his brother, William. The doctor found upon examination that the skull was fractured, the shoulder out of joint, the right ankle broken and other internal injuries. Mr. Sidey never regained consciousness, and passed away at 6 o'clock that evening.

John Sidey was seriously injured by the same timber, a number of ribs were broken, his right lung punctured and a general shaking up. Willoughby Nesbitt was thrown some fifteen feet and slightly injured and Alex Royal received a few scratches. It was a miracle they were not killed."

Richard Sidey's wife had died twelve years previously and he had one son, age 12.

John Sidey married Christina Melville who is remembered in the history books as the person who saw the first train arrive in Creemore and also the last one. Their daughter, Annie, married Bob More and their son, Allan, was village constable for a number of years. Elizabeth or Lizzie married George Montgomery and lived west of Creemore about a mile. The Montgomery family have been mail carriers for many, many years and a daughter, Elizabeth Beattie, and her husband carry on the family tradition. Bob Montgomery is our crossing guard at the main corner and general helper about town. Wheldale Sidey farmed on his father's place before selling out and becoming Creemore's general handyman and constable. He died in 1961.

NOTES
1. Hogg's Map of the County of Simcoe, 1871.
2. 1871 Census, Nottawasaga, C-9962.
3. Creemore Star, July 13, 1916, p. 1.

THE STEED FAMILY

The Steed name has been well known around Creemore for more than 140 years. The account of the history of the Anglican church tells us how Michael was one of the main carpenters who built it. As a matter of fact it was probably the first job he had here.[1]

Michael Steed originally came from Ballyanhinch, Ireland, near Belfast. He came first, not to Canada, but to the state of New York. After a short time there he moved on, and with his tool chest (he was a cabinet maker) and some supplies made his way with a team of oxen to Upper Canada, or Ontario in 1854. It has been said that he stopped in Mulmur long enough to find it not to his liking and then moved on to Lot 7, Concession 4 in Nottawasaga, jut to the south and west of Creemore.

Michael's wife was Eliza De Coursier. Five children were born to this couple: Thomas, who died as a child, William, George, Janie, and another Thomas.

Eliza died in 1863 and not long after Michael married Mary Weatherup. Their family consisted of Alfred, Robert, Isabella and Christopher. Alfred and Christopher died as very young children.

As with many other pioneer families not many of the children remained in the area. William went to Hamilton; George, a blacksmith moved to British Columbia. Jane married William John Bell of Creemore and moved to Michigan; Thomas lived at Revelstoke, British Columbia; Isabella married Harry De Coursier and their family lived in such far flung places as Scotland and Prince Albert, Saskatchewan.

This leaves Robert, who remained on the family homestead. He and his wife, Ada Dartnell, had sons, Ed, Jack and Tom. Ed began his teaching career in Creemore before moving on to Sarnia and Ottawa. Tom and Jack remained at Creemore and it is Jack's son, Jim, who carries on the family name. One of his sisters, Eleanor Wines, lives in Creemore and the other sister, Norma Lawler, is at Markdale.

NOTES

1. The information about this family comes from Jim Steed, Eleanor Wines, and <u>Centennial Stories</u>, pp 49-50.

THE WEBSTER FAMILY

The Webster story begins in County Wexford, a lush and prosperous area on the south east coast of Ireland. There, an extended Webster family lived on a farm in the townland of Garrybritt near the small town of Enniscorthy. Life was serene and good. Although Catholics and Protestants had different rights they lived together in harmony as good neighbours should.

Suddenly in the 1790s, the differences became an issue. The issues were legitimate, without a doubt, and there was more to it than just religion, a matter that is usually emphasized. The economics of the time also were points of dissension. The coals of rebellion were fanned and one spring night in 1798 passions broke into flames. This was more than a figure of speech. The Webster home was one of the first set on fire. Farm animals were destroyed, crops and tools ruined.

The Webster family escaped from the burning inferno and hid in ditches and hedgerows. A couple of days later, while attempting to escape into safe hands, the father, Robert, was murdered in front of his family on Enniscorthy bridge. Several pikes were thrust into him and he was thrown into the river. The rest of the family were able to get away.

The rebellion died down with little resolved, but, as you can imagine, the situation was none too pleasant. By 1812, nine Webster brothers and sisters, and possibly their mother, made their way to Canada crossing the Atlantic in a sailing vessel. They gradually established themselves in Leeds County in what is Eastern Ontario.

It was from there that Edward and George, grandsons of Robert, and sons of William, made their way to Creemore. As has been recounted, they played a major role in the development of Creemore.

It must have been a traumatic day in 1862 when Edward was served notice of foreclosure. What was he to do, a man with a wife and eight young children? They packed up and left their busy, happy home beside the Mad River and moved to Toronto.

The old Toronto street directories give us an account of a very different lifestyle than the one they had been living. They moved about every two years and Edward took on a different job just about as often. His wife, Mary, set up a dressmaking business and was helped by daughters, Caroline and Kate. It appears that Edward had lost all heart and ambition.

In 1870 sons, Frank and Wellington, joined the migration to Michigan. Frank remained there until 1900 when he moved to California. Wellington returned to Toronto but after 1871 his whereabouts has not been found. A note left in Alice Emmett's family history papers suggests he became a professional gambler.

Edward and Mary's daughter, Elizabeth, married in Etobicoke where many of her descendants still live. Her sister, Caroline, remained in Toronto but did not marry.

In 1886 Edward and his wife moved to California, probably Pasadena. It seems that the youngest, Arthur, was already there and although Edward was getting along in years he may have seen opportunities for a better life in a warmer climate. Then, by 1900, Edward, Mary and family, Frank, Arthur and Susan were to be found in Bakersfield, California. The sons were busy with a garage and selling mining equipment. Susan ran a boarding house. Unfortunately Arthur was killed in a car accident in 1908 leaving a wife and young daughter. Edward died in 1902 and was buried in Pasadena.

Son, George, became a civil engineer, becoming one of the higher-ups for the Canadian Pacific Railway. He lived out the most of his life in Vancouver, British Columbia. Sister, Kate, may have died at a young age but information about her is not available. Edward's wife, Mary, later went to Vancouver and died there.

Edward's brother, George, remained in Creemore, and in 1876, emulating his older brother, surveyed the village of Websterville a mile or so west of Creemore. He established a saw mill on the Mad River and sold lots. While he didn't go bankrupt, he never became rich either, in his attempt to found a village. He and his wife retired to a pleasant little brick house on Caroline Street in Creemore. Of their family of six, only one remained in Websterville. (A son, Walter, was killed in a mill accident at age fourteen.) The son who remained was Frank, also referred to a F. E. His grandson, Fran, along with his family lives on part of the old family farm. Frank's granddaughters, Ruth Hughes and Helen Blackburn, along with their families also live in the Creemore area today.

SOURCES

BOOKS

Akenson, Donald Harmon. The Irish in Ontario: A Study in Rural History, Montreal and Kingston: McGill-Queen's University Press, 1984.

Ardagh, Henry R. Life of Sir James Gowan 1815-1909, Toronto: University of Toronto Press, 1911.

Conway, Sean Gerard J. The Spread of the Loyal Orange Lodge Through Ontario 1830-1900, Thesis # 19, Archives of Ontario.

Davis, Wm H. Genealogical and Historical Records of the Davis and Galloway Families 1822-1947.

Doherty, G. F. B., Rev. A Brief Historical Survey of the Parish of St. Luke, Toronto, 1870-1955. The Archives, Diocese of Toronto, Anglican Church of Canada, Toronto.

Douglas, Agnes J. Dowling Family History and the History of the First Roman Catholic Church and the First Separate School in Nottawasaga, Collingwood July, 1994.

Eagle, A. G. Methodist Beginnings in Nottawasaga Township (Simcoe County) Especially as it Relates to the Present Circuit of Creemore), Toronto: University of Toronto Press, 1950.

Emmett, Alice. Creemore Tweedsmuir History, in Creemore Public Library.

Gates, Lillian. The Land Policies of Upper Canada, Toronto: University of Toronto Press, 1968.

Gowan, James H. B. Genealogy of the Clan Gowan, Iver, Bucks., England, 1978.

Hargrave, Helen Has the Bell Rung Yet?, Creemore, 1979.

Heslip, Jack;
Thomson, Thelma;
Dickenson Marion The Centennial History of St. John's United Church, Creemore,Ontario, 1886-1986.

Hunter, A. F. A History of Simcoe County, Barrie: The Historical Committee of Simcoe County, 1909

Lambert, R. S. The Gothic Rectory, Creemore, 1971.

Langtry, Margaret. Two Hundred Years of Langtry History 1761-1960, Lake Forest, Illinois: Arthur C. Langtry, July, 1961.

Merriman, Brenda. Genealogy in Ontario: Searching the Records, 3rd Edition, Toronto: The Ontario Genealogical Society, 1996.

Maynard, Edward (ed.) A Glimpse of Creemore's Past, Creemore Centennial Committee, 1989.

Renfree, Harry A. Heritage and Horizon: The Baptist Story in Canada, Mississauga: Canadian Baptist Federation, 1988.

Smith, C. B. Centennial Stories of Creemore, Nottawasaga, Their People, a Collection Of Anecdotes, Family Histories and Some Selections of the Writings of C. B. Smith, Creemore, 1967.

Smith, C. B. 100 Years of History: St. Luke's, Creemore, 1855-1955.

Smith, W. L. The Pioneers of Old Ontario, Toronto: George N. Morang, 1923.

120

Spiers, Mrs. John.	The Giffen History from 1842 to 1970, 1957, revised in 1970 by Mrs. Scott Robinson.
Thomson, Samuel.	Reminiscences of a Canadian Pioneer, Toronto: Hunter, Rose & Company, 1884.
Walker, Frank.	Four Whistles to Wood-Up, Toronto: Upper Canada Railway Society, 1953.
Webster, F. E. (ed.)	Nottawasaga: The Outburst of the Iroquois, Creemore: The Historical Committee, Nottawasaga Centennial Celebration, 1934.
Williams, David.	The Origin of the Names of the Post Offices of Simcoe County, Toronto: William Briggs, 1906.

ARTICLES

Fraser, Mrs. H. E.	"Early days of the Baptist Church in Creemore," The Canadian Baptist, September 1, 1967.
Houston, Cecil H.	"The Spread of the Loyal Orange Lodge Through Ontario, 1830-1900," Smyth, William J.A paper presented at the 1978 Canadian History Association Meeting, London. At the Archives of Ontario.
Saunders	"The Story of Orangeism." A pamphlet. at the Archives of Ontario.
Seibert, Lou.	"The Land Surveys of Ontario 1750-1980," Cartographica, vol. 17, No. 3, Autumn 1980. At the Archives of Ontario.

NEWSPAPERS

Creemore Star-microfilm at Creemore Public Library.

Collingwood Saturday News, microfilm at Collingwood Public Library.

The Examiner, Barrie, microfilm at Simcoe County Archives, Midhurst.

Northern Advance, Barrie, microfilm at Simcoe County Archives, Midhurst.

Orangeville Sun, Orangeville, microfilm at Dufferin County Archives.

MICROFILMS, MICROFICHE

Assessments for Nottawasaga Township, on microfilm at Simcoe County Archives, Midhurst.

1861 Census, Nottawasaga, # 1073, microfilm at Collingwood Public Library.

1871 Census, Nottawasaga, # C-9962, microfilm at Collingwood Public Library.

Griffith's Valuation, microfiche, Toronto Reference Library, Toronto.

Land Petitions, W 7/6 Vol. 542, at the Archives of Ontario

Land Records, Nottawasaga, MS 658, Reel 348, microfilm, Archives of Ontario.

Ontario Marriage Registrations, MS 932, Reel 17 (for Sarah Nalty), microfilm at the Archives of Ontario.

Thomas Kelly's Diary, Survey of Nottawasaga, 1832, microfilm MS 924, Reel 18, Archives of Ontario.

MAPS

Creemore: The Property of Edward Webster by William Gibbard, Dec., 1853, at the Archives of Ontario, C 295-1-41-0-1.

Hogg's Map of the County of Simcoe 1871, at the Archives of Ontario, John Hogg, A-10.

Archelaus Tupper, A Plan of Nottawasaga, dated at the City of Toronto, May 5th, 1837. At Simcoe County Archives, Midhurst.

Village of Creemore...part of Lots 9 & 8 in the 4th and 5th concessions of the Township of Nottawasaga. The property of E. Webster, Esq. Surveyed by W. Sanders, P. L. S., 1861. At the Land Registry Office, Barrie and in the possession of Donald Webster.

ORIGINAL RECORDS

Creemore School Board Minute Books, stored at Clearview Municipal Office, Stayner.

Nottawasaga Land Records, Land Registry Office, Barrie.

Orange Lodge transfer Certificates, Purple Hill Lodge #193, Creemore Lodge #704, at Simcoe County Archives, Midhurst.

Rankin Field Notes, Survey of Nottawasaga, Ministry of Natural Resources, Office of the Surveyor General, 2nd Floor, North Tower, 300 Water Street, Box 7000, Peterborough, Ontario, K9J 3C7.

Royal Arch Purple Lodge, No. 704, Creemore, members 1856-1943, minutes 1860-1950, at Creemore Public Library.

NOTE
The spelling and punctuation in some quotations have been changed to clarify meaning.

INDEX

128